book is to be

TRAVERSE
THEATRE

Traverse Theatre Company

Shetland Saga
by Sue Glover

cast in order of speaking

Brit	Elaine MacKenzie Ellis
Angel	Eric Barlow
Mena	Lesley Hart
Svetan	Cas Harkins
Natka	Anne Lacey
Hoover	Simon Scott
Manson	David Gallacher
Andronov	David Gallacher
Musician	Annalie Hayward

director	Philip Howard
designer	Mark Leese
lighting designer	Ben Ormerod
composer	Paul Johnston
dialect coach	Ros Steen
choreographer	Jane
stage manager	Gavi
deputy stage manager	Klare
assistant stage manager	Laurc
wardrobe supervisor	Lynn
wardrobe assistants	Caitlin Blair & Miriam Dumie

First performed at the Traverse Theatre
Friday 28 July 2000

TRAVERSE THEATRE

One of the most important theatres in Britain The Observer

Edinburgh's **Traverse Theatre** is Scotland's new writing theatre, with a 37 year record of excellence. With quality, award-winning productions and programming, the Traverse receives accolades at home and abroad from audiences and critics alike.

The Traverse has an unrivalled reputation for producing contemporary theatre of the highest quality, invention and energy, commissioning and supporting writers from Scotland and around the world and facilitating numerous script development workshops, rehearsed readings and public writing workshops. The Traverse aims to produce several major new theatre productions plus a Scottish touring production each year. It is unique in Scotland in its exclusive dedication to new writing, providing the infrastructure, professional support and expertise to ensure the development of a sustainable and relevant theatre culture for Scotland and the UK.

Traverse Theatre Company productions have been seen worldwide including London, Toronto, Budapest and New York. Recent touring successes in Scotland include PERFECT DAYS by Liz Lochhead, PASSING PLACES by Stephen Greenhorn, HIGHLAND SHORTS, HERITAGE by Nicola McCartney and LAZYBED by Iain Crichton Smith. PERFECT DAYS also played the Vaudeville Theatre in London's West End in 1999. In 2000 the Traverse co-produced Michel Tremblay's SOLEMN MASS FOR A FULL MOON IN SUMMER with London's Barbican Centre, with performances in both Edinburgh and London.

The Traverse can be relied upon to produce more
good-quality new plays than any other Fringe venue
Daily Telegraph

During the Edinburgh Festival the Traverse is one of the most important venues with world class premieres playing daily in the two theatre spaces. The Traverse regularly wins awards at the Edinburgh Festival Fringe, including recent *Scotsman Fringe Firsts* for Traverse productions KILL THE OLD TORTURE THEIR YOUNG by David Harrower and PERFECT DAYS by Liz Lochhead.

An essential element of the Traverse Company's activities takes place within the educational sector, concentrating on the process of playwriting for young people. The Traverse flagship education project CLASS ACT offers young people in schools the opportunity to work with theatre professionals and see their work performed on the Traverse stage. In addition the Traverse Young Writers group, led by professional playwrights, has been running for over three years and meets weekly.

Sue Glover

Sue Glover is one of Scotland's foremost playwrights whose plays have been produced worldwide to enormous critical and audience acclaim. *Bondagers*, her last play for the Traverse, is a modern Scottish classic. Her other plays include *The Straw Chair* and *The Seal Wife*. Sue also writes for radio and television.

Sue Glover and the Traverse gratefully thank the actors who contributed to the development stage of the play:

Kate Dickie, Ron Donachie, Paul Thomas Hickey, Louise Ironside, Anne Lacey, Iain Macrae, Derek Riddell.

BIOGRAPHIES

Eric Barlow (Angel): Trained: Queen Margaret College in Edinburgh. For the Traverse: THE SPECULATOR, HERITAGE and THE ARCHITECT. Other theatre work includes: RUG COMES TO SHUV (Theatre Gerrard Phillipe, Paris), PORTRAIT OF A WOMAN, THE SUICIDE (Communicado), MACBETH, PETER PAN, THREE SISTERS, THE SHAUGHRAUN, MOTHER COURAGE, HAMLET, MUCH ADO ABOUT NOTHING, THE MERCHANT OF VENICE, THE CAUCASIAN CHALK CIRCLE, WAITING FOR GODOT, OUR COUNTRY'S GOOD, HANSEL AND GRETEL, SLEEPING BEAUTY, THE TAMING OF THE SHREW, BEAUTY AND THE BEAST, MERLIN THE MAGNIFICENT, THE PRINCESS AND THE GOBLIN, ARSENIC AND OLD LACE, MERLIN – SEARCH FOR THE GRAIL, MIRANDOLINA (Royal Lyceum), ROMEO AND JULIET, MACBETH, LOVE BUT HER (Brunton), THE SALT WOUND (7:84), THE WISHING TREE (Wiseguise), THE HARP AND THE VIOLET, THE PRINCESS AND THE GOBLIN (Dundee Rep), THE CHIC MURRAY STORY (Pavilion), OH! WHAT A LOVELY WAR (Wildcat), GRAND MAGIC, THE SCHOOL FOR SCANDAL (Perth), THE MAGISTRATE, THE NORMAN CONQUESTS, DEATH OF A SALESMAN, DOMINION OF FANCY (Pitlochry Festival Theatre), WHEN HAIR WAS LONG AND LIFE WAS SHORT, AND ME WI'AH BAD LEG TAE (Borderline). Eric's film work includes: ORPHANS (Antonine/Greenbridge), MY LIFE SO FAR (Miramax), THE INITIATION, HARD NUT – A LOVE STORY (Ideal World). Television work includes: THE YOUNG PERSON'S GUIDE TO BECOMING A ROCK STAR (Channel 4), MURDER ROOMS – THE DARK BEGINNINGS OF SHERLOCK HOLMES, MCCALLUM, TAGGART, DR FINDLAY (STV) RAB C NESBITT (BBC). His radio work includes: SWANSONG, HYDRO, TALL DROLL, AFTER ICARUS.

David Gallacher (Manson/Andronov): Following a sabbatical of ten years, when he was a partner in an arboricultural practice, David's recent theatre work includes: SOLEMN MASS FOR A FULL MOON IN SUMMER for the Traverse; THE DREAM TRAIN (Magnetic North) and FREE ROPE (Edinburgh International Festival for the Saltire Society). Recent film and television work includes: COMPLICITY, TAGGART and REBUS - BLACK AND BLUE.

Cas Harkins (Svetan): Trained: RSAMD. Theatre includes PHAEDRA'S LOVE (Gate & Citizens'); ROMEO AND JULIET (Chester Gateway); HERACLES (Gate); MACBETH (Cage). Television includes STONE COLD, BLISS, THE BILL, CASUALTY, LONDON'S BURNING. Film includes: THE ACID HOUSE. Cas will also be appearing in a new BBC2 series TINSEL TOWN due to be screened in the autumn.

Lesley Hart (*Mena*): Graduating this year from RSAMD. Final year productions include STAGS AND HENS and THE ART OF SUCCESS. Lesley has worked with Haddo Productions and Open Window Productions, a theatre company formed by RSAMD students in 1998. Recent theatre performances include HUSHABYE MOUNTAIN, ROAD and THE ODD COUPLE (Open Window Productions).

Annalie Hayward (Musician): Trained: Trinity College of Music, London. Annalie is originally from Weisdale on the west side of Shetland, although she has lived all over the UK. She has played the violin for 15 years and recently moved back to Shetland where she has developed her interest in traditional fiddle. Annalie works as a music teacher for children with special educational needs and hopes to study music therapy at post graduate level.

Philip Howard (director): Philip trained at the Royal Court Theatre, London, on the Regional Theatre Young Director Scheme from 1988-90. He was Associate Director at the Traverse from 1993-96, and has been Artistic Director since 1996. Productions for the Traverse include: LOOSE ENDS, BROTHERS OF THUNDER, EUROPE, KNIVES IN HENS (also Bush Theatre), THE ARCHITECT, FAITH HEALER, WORMWOOD, LAZYBED, THE CHIC NERDS, KILL THE OLD TORTURE THEIR YOUNG, HERITAGE, THE SPECULATOR, HIGHLAND SHORTS and SOLEMN MASS FOR A FULL MOON IN SUMMER (with Ros Steen). Philip's other theatre includes HIPPOLYTUS (Arts Theatre Cambridge), ENTERTAINING MR SLOANE (Royal, Northampton) and SOMETHING ABOUT US (Lyric Hammersmith Studio).

Paul Johnston (composer): Has fronted the band ROCK SALT & NAILS for the last 10 years, writing contemporary songs and music inspired by the traditional music of Shetland. This is the first time he has worked with the Traverse.

Anne Lacey (*Natka*): For the Traverse: BONDAGERS, THE STRAW CHAIR, THE SILVER SPRIG. For Communicado: MARY QUEEN OF SCOTS GOT HER HEAD CHOPPED OFF, THE HOUSE WITH THE GREEN SHUTTERS, JOCK TAMSONS BAIRNS, THE CONE GATHERERS, TALL TALES. Anne has worked with many other companies including the Citizens', Old Vic, Dundee Rep, Raindog, Tron and most recently in VICTORIA for the RSC. Television includes: 3 series as Esme in HAMISH MACBETH, DEACON BRODIE, DOCTOR FINLAY, KNOWING THE SCORE, RAB C. NESBITT, SWEET NOTHINGS, SHOOT FOR THE SUN, WILDFLOWERS. Film includes: MY LIFE SO FAR, THIS YEAR'S LOVE, COCOZZA'S WAY. Shorts include: MIRROR, MIRROR, NAN. Radio includes many short stories, plays and comedy with BBC Radio.

Mark Leese (designer): For the Traverse: THE SPECULATOR, KILL THE OLD TORTURE THEIR YOUNG, KNIVES IN HENS, THE CHIC NERDS, GRETA, ANNA WEISS, WIDOWS, FAITH HEALER, THE HOPE SLIDE, BROTHERS OF THUNDER. Other recent work includes: FROGS (Royal National Theatre); THE PLAYBOY OF THE WESTERN WORLD, A FAMILY AFFAIR (Dundee Rep); MARTIN YESTERDAY (Royal Exchange, Manchester); A WEEKEND IN ENGLAND (Gateway, Chester); THE GREEKS (Theatre Babel); PARALLEL LINES (Theatre Cryptic); BORN GUILTY, THE WAR IN HEAVEN, THE GRAPES OF WRATH, THE SALT WOUND, ANTIGONE (7:84); ON GOLDEN POND (Royal Lyceum); BLACK COMEDY, PUBLIC EYE (Watford Palace). Film work includes: HOME (CH4, BAFTA winner); HIDDEN, NIGHT SWIMMER, BILLIE AND ZORBA, SPITTING DISTANCE, GOLDEN WEDDING, CANDY FLOSS (BBC), PASTURES NEW, GOOD DAY FOR THE BAD GUYS, RUBY (STV), CALIFORNIA SUNSHINE, HEART AND SOLE (CH4). Mark is Design Associate at the Traverse.

Elaine MacKenzie Ellis (*Brit*): For the Traverse: DANNY 306 + ME (4 EVER). Other theatre includes: TEECHERS (Byre); ALADDIN (Adam Smith); THE WIZARD OF OZ (Citizens'); RUMPELSTILTSKIN (Cumbernauld); PYGMALION (Royal Lyceum); THE PRINCESS & THE GOBLIN (MacRobert). Television work includes: RAB C NESBITT, ATHLETICO PARTICK (Comedy Unit); TAGGART (STV); PARA HANDY (BBC). Film includes MY LIFE SO FAR, MY NAME IS JOE, THE CUP. Radio work includes: HAND IN GLOVE, BLUE WHOLE FISH (BBC).

Simon Scott (Hoover): For the Traverse: LUCY'S PLAY. Other theatre includes: FILUMENA (Piccadilly); THE DOCTOR'S DILEMMA (Almeida); ONE FLEW OVER THE CUCKOO'S NEST (Centreline). For the Royal National Theatre: SHE STOOPS TO CONQUER, CITIZEN OF THE WORLD, THE HOT SUMMER, A CHORUS OF DISAPPROVAL, HAMLET, KING LEAR, ANTHONY AND CLEOPATRA, ENTERTAINING STRANGERS, CYMBELINE, THE TEMPEST, A WINTERS TALE (& world tour), THE MADNESS OF GEORGE III (& world tour), OEDIPUS PLAYS (& Epidaurus), THE PRIME OF MISS JEAN BRODIE (Strand), LES LIAISONS DANGEREUSES (RSC at The Ambassadors). Other theatre includes: Birmingham Rep, Perth Theatre, Compass and Derby Playhouse. Work for television includes: BIG BAD WORLD, KID IN THE CORNER, TAGGART, FOSTERING EVIL, THE DEMON HEADMASTER, INSPECTOR MORSE, CASUALTY, THE BILL, THE REVEREND JOLLY, BETWEEN THE LINES, TAKE THE HIGH ROAD, ADVOCATES 2. Film includes: WHATEVER HAPPENED TO HAROLD SMITH, A PASSION FOR LIFE, COLD FISH, BEGINNERS LUCK, THE FINAL CURTAIN. Radio includes:

THE DOCTOR'S DILEMMA, THE OEDIPUS PLAYS, BESIDE THE OCEAN OF TIME, THE GOOD THIEF, THE SERPENT'S BACK, THE WALL.

Ros Steen (dialect coach): Trained: RSAMD. Co-directed SOLEMN MASS FOR A FULL MOON IN SUMMER for the Traverse. As voice coach for the Traverse: KING OF THE FIELDS, HIGHLAND SHORTS, FAMILY, HERITAGE, KILL THE OLD TORTURE THEIR YOUNG, THE CHIC NERDS, GRETA, LAZYBED, KNIVES IN HENS, PASSING PLACES, BONDAGERS, ROAD TO NIRVANA, SHARP SHORTS, MARISOL, GRACE IN AMERICA, BROTHERS OF THUNDER. Other theatre work includes: OLEANNA, SUMMIT CONFERENCE, KRAPPS'S LAST TAPE, THE DYING GAOL, CONVERSATION WITH A CUPBOARD MAN, EVA PERON, LONG DAY'S JOURNEY INTO NIGHT (Citizens'); PLAYBOY OF THE WESTERN WORLD, A MIDSUMMER NIGHT'S DREAM (Dundee Rep); SEA URCHINS (Tron & Dundee Rep); HOME, TRANSATLANTIC, THE HANGING TREE, LAUNDRY and ENTERTAINING ANGELS (LookOut); ODYSSEUS THUMP (West Yorkshire Playhouse); MYTHS OF THE NEAR FUTURE (untitled); BEUL NAM BREUG (Tosg Theatar Gaidhlig); TRAVELS WITH MY AUNT, THE PRICE (Brunton); TRAINSPOTTING (G & J Productions); HOW TO SAY GOODBYE, BABYCAKES (Clyde Unity); ABIGAIL'S PARTY (Perth Rep); LOVERS, PYGMALION, OUR COUNTRY'S GOOD (Royal Lyceum); SUNSET SONG (TAG). Film includes: GREGORY'S TWO GIRLS, STELLA DOES TRICKS and STAND AND DELIVER. Television includes: MONARCH OF THE GLEN, HAMISH MACBETH, LOOKING AFTER JOJO, ST ANTHONY'S DAY OFF and CHANGING STEP.

Ben Ormerod (lighting designer): For the Traverse: MAN TO MAN, SHARP SHORTS, PASSING PLACES. Ben began his career with Andrew Visnevski's Cherub company, touring Europe with productions such as Kafka's THE TRIAL before lighting for Deborah Warner's Kick Theatre. As well as designing theatre, opera and dance for the national companies, reps and touring companies throughout the UK, Ben has worked extensively abroad including Greece, Slovenia, Japan, and most recently Ireland where he lit THE BEAUTY QUEEN OF LEENANE for Druid Theatre which he has since taken to London, Broadway, Sydney and Toronto. Forthcoming work includes REMEMBRANCE OF THINGS PAST (Royal National Theatre), HENRY V (RSC), THE BENCH (Theatro Synchrono, Athens) and a new dance piece by Didi Veldman (Gulbenkian Theatre, Lisbon). Ben is also currently lighting The Calico Textiles Museum, Ahmedebad.

For generous help on
Shetland Saga
the Traverse thanks:

Walkers• Sheraton Grand Hotel • Dalton Demolition UK.
Ltd.• Fishers of Leith • Varis Engineering, Forres
Ann Duncan, Edinburgh Butterfly and Insect World
The Edinburgh Cake Shop • Geo. Henderson Ltd
BLF

LEVER BROTHERS for wardrobe care

Sets, props and costumes for
Shetland Saga
created by Traverse Workshops
(funded by the National Lottery)

scenic artist Monique Jones
painters Julie Kirsop, Jenny Lau, Siobhan O'Neill
carpentry workshop placement Maja Flygare
placement Alasdair McKay

production photography Kevin Low
print photography Euan Myles

SPONSORSHIP

Sponsorship income enables the Traverse to commission and produce new plays and offer audiences a diverse and exciting programme of events throughout the year.

We would like to thank the following companies for their support throughout the year:

BANK OF SCOTLAND

B B C Scotland **artism**

CORPORATE ASSOCIATE SCHEME

LEVEL ONE
Balfour Beatty
Scottish Life the PENSION company
United Distillers & Vintners

LEVEL TWO
Laurence Smith -
Wine Merchants
NB Information
Willis Corroon Scotland Ltd
Wired Nomad

LEVEL THREE
Alistir Tait FGA -
Antiques & Fine Jewellery
Nicholas Groves Raines -
Architects
McCabe Partnership -
Chartered Accountants
KPMG
Scottish Post Office Board

With thanks to

Navy Blue Design, print designers for the Traverse and George Stewarts the printers.

Purchase of the Traverse Box Office, computer network and technical and training equipment has been made possible with money from The Scottish Arts Council National Lottery Fund.

THE SCOTTISH ARTS COUNCIL
National Lottery Fund

The Traverse Theatre's work would not be possible without the support of

THE SCOTTISH ARTS COUNCIL **·EDINBVRGH·**
THE CITY OF EDINBURGH COUNCIL

The Traverse receives financial assistance for its educational and development work from

John Lewis Partnership, Peggy Ramsay Foundation, Binks Trust, The Yapp Charitable Trusts, The Bulldog Prinsep Theatrical Trust, Calouste Gulbenkian Foundation, Gannochy Trust, Gordon Fraser Charitable Trust, The Garfield Weston Foundation, The Paul Hamlyn Foundation, JSP Pollitzer Charitable Trust.

The Education Institute of Scotland, supporting arts projects produced by and for children.

Charity No. SC002368

Sue Glover

SHETLAND SAGA

A Nick Hern Book

Shetland Saga first published in Great Britain in 2000
as an original paperback by Nick Hern Books Limited,
14 Larden Road, London W3 7ST, in association with the
Traverse Theatre, Edinburgh

Typeset by Country Setting, Kingsdown, Kent CT14 8ES
Printed and bound in Great Britain by Athenaeum Press Ltd,
Gateshead, Tyne and Wear

A CIP catalogue record for this book is available from
the British Library

ISBN 1 85459 607 1

For Philip

*With many thanks to those I met
in Shetland, Ullapool and Aberdeen*

Gordon Williamson, Georgi Spasov
Yenka Klishin, John McMeechan, Ksenja Howat
Duncan and Greta Stewart, Donald Macleod,
Tony Hughes, Sid Hall and Kaye Gilmore

Characters

Shetlanders

MENA (Philomena Jameson), *young Shetland girl, hotel receptionist.*

HOOVER JIM, *Mena's uncle. He has a small hotel right on the quayside, and a 'sea and land' taxi service, and acts as general supplier to all the Klondyker ships.*

BRIT, *local girl who also works in the hotel.*

NORRIE MANSON, *local man, trade-union representative.*

Bulgarians

SVETAN, *ship's engineer, youngish.*

ANGEL (*pronounced Angle by the Bulgarians*), *another engineer. Very large, bear of a man.*

NATKA, *a fish-gutter, i.e., she works as a gutter and packer but also – especially as skeleton crew – as cleaner, washer-up. Lowly position, but a very independent person.*

COLONEL, *member of Bulgarian secret police.*

Norrie Manson and Colonel to be played by same actor.

This text went to press before the opening night, and may therefore differ slightly from the play as performed.

ACT ONE

The acting space must seem as limitless as possible: the quay, and the Ludmilla. An impression of her size – the hull looming above us. The gangplank is important. It concertinas (ramsay ladder style), as does its rope and metal handrail. Mostly the contraption is never completely unfolded – sways alarmingly, requires some gymnastics to leap from quay to ramp, and vice versa.

The set must not be absolute, it must suggest ship, (and scenes on board), quayside, and the quayside hotel/bar. But ship and/or shore scenes should, at any necessary point, be able to invade and utilise what space there is.

And beyond, behind, the Ludmilla, there is a sense of sea and sky. At night, lights from other vessels, either out to sea, or nearby in the docks.

Scene One

ANGEL *wheels on an old bike, with large panniers at the sides and front, stuffed with objects. He unhooks the pump, or starts to unload.*

BRIT (*voice off*). Hey – you –

  ANGEL *pays no heed, busy with the junk.*

  BRIT *enters, tea-towel or something in hand, straight from the bar of the dockside hotel where she works.*

  Hey – You – Klondyker! That's not your bike.

ANGEL. Yes. Mine.

BRIT. No. Mine. My kid brother's, to be exact.

ANGEL. I found this –

BRIT. You think bikes are usually painted that way? He did it up himself.

MENA *enters.*

MENA. Brit! What's going on out there?

SVETAN *has appeared on deck by now.*

BRIT (*to* ANGEL). All you Russkies are the same.

SVETAN (*to* ANGEL, *in Bulgarian*). Angel, what's going on down there?

ANGEL (*to* SVETAN, *in Bulgarian*). She is calling me a thief. A *Russian* thief!

MENA (*to* BRIT). They're not Russkies, they're Bulgarian.

SVETAN (*to* ANGEL, *in Bulgarian*). Where d'you get the bike?

ANGEL (*to* SVETAN, *in Bulgarian*). Don't *you* start, for Crissake.

BRIT (*to* MENA). Oh, for Crissake –

MENA. Keep it down, Brit –

SVETAN (*to* ANGEL, *Bulgarian*). Angel: where d'you get the bike?

BRIT (*to* MENA). He's pinched Donnie's bike.

MENA. We can hear you back there in the bar.

BRIT. Good! Maybe some of those other light-fingered Klondyk –

MENA. Shut. Up.

BRIT. I helped Donnie buy that bike! I helped him paint it!

MENA. You think this guy jogged all the way up the Old North Road and pinched it from your back door?

SVETAN (*to* ANGEL, *in Bulgarian*). What are they saying?

ANGEL (*to* SVETAN, *in Bulgarian*). She still thinks I'm a thief. A Rooskie thief!

SVETAN (*to* ANGEL, *in Bulgarian*). Jesus, Angel, you never pinched a bike?

BRIT (*to* MENA). It's been missing for days.

ANGEL (*to* SVETAN, *in Bulgarian*). I found it on the dump. I found it on the dump – okay?

MENA. Some joyrider's got bored and chucked it on the dump. Look, it's filthy – the paint's all chipped!

BRIT. So?

Fast.

MENA. This guy – the big one – he does business with Hoover –

BRIT. So? –

MENA. They're buddies –

BRIT. So?

MENA (*gives up on this tack; to* ANGEL). Where did you find it?

ANGEL. Yes. The dump. Inside, not outside by gate. Inside. Inside, on top of rubbish. Today. Afternoon today.

MENA. Look, I'm awfully sorry, but it belongs to her wee brother. I'm sorry, it was pinched – stolen – a few days ago. I'm really sorry!

BRIT. Not as sorry as Donnie.

MENA (*to* BRIT). Look, he speaks English, watch what you're saying.

ANGEL *has clumsily started to remove his booty from the bike panniers.*

MENA (*to* BRIT). Apologise.

BRIT. What for?

MENA. Well, at least buy him a drink next time he's in the bar.

ANGEL *looks very hopeful.*

BRIT. They don't come into the bar, not this lot (*Indicating the Ludmilla and crew.*) – they're skint.

MENA. And don't call them Russians, they're Bulgarian.You should know they're Bulgarian, they've been here months now.

ANGEL (*calling to* SVETAN, *in Bulgarian*). What do you think? Not bad, eh? Not bad at all. Very nice girls, in fact.

SVETAN (*to* ANGEL, *in Bulgarian*). Too young for you.

BRIT (*taking the bike; to* ANGEL). Sorry about this.

NATKA *comes out on deck, for a smoke.*

ANGEL. *I* am sorry. Very sorry.

He kisses her hand, and arm, despite the bike and his unpacked booty getting in the way, goes on to kiss MENA*'s hand.*

BRIT. He'll be up to your oxters in a minute!

SVETAN (*to* ANGEL, *in Bulgarian*). Angel, put her down, you'll get arrested.

ANGEL (*to both girls*). Now, you come for coffee – you – and you?

MENA *is looking at* SVETAN.

BRIT. No, no, thanks all the same. Got to get back to work.

She is going, ahead of MENA, *with the bike.*

(*Calling* MENA *to come too.*) Mena! Hoover'll skin us alive.

ANGEL (*calling after* BRIT). Tomorrow – come for coffee.

BRIT (*to* MENA). I'll put the bike round the back.

BRIT *goes, with bike.*

MENA (*includes* SVETAN *in her goodbye*). Good luck – for the Ludmilla! Good luck!

BRIT (*voice off, calling, exasperated*). Phil-o-meeeeena!

MENA *goes.*

NATKA. Good luck! Huh! We don't have luck! And we don't have any coffee.

SVETAN *comes down onto the quay.*

ANGEL (*to* SVETAN, *Bulgarian*). Very nice, eh? Very very nice.

SVETAN *examines* ANGEL*'s 'junk'.*

ANGEL. One for you – one for me . . . The blonde one's (*Blonde, plump, slim, whatever describes* BRIT.) something, isn't she? Lots of make-up. Most of these Shetland girls don't wear make-up – it's there in the shops – shelves and shelves of it, all colours, not expensive, either – but they hardly ever put it on!

SVETAN *ignores all this.*

What's this? What's it for?

ANGEL. She had glitter on her cheeks. I like that, it makes me think of . . . dancing . . . discos . . .

NATKA. Elvis!

They don't hear her. She goes.

SVETAN (*pulls something from pile; irritable*). And this? What on earth can you do with this?

ANGEL. The other one, the quiet one, I think she's Hoover's niece. No make-up at all!

SVETAN. And this?

ANGEL. The blonde (*Tall, dark, whatever, describes* BRIT.) one works behind the bar.

SVETAN (*exasperated – holding up some kitsch knick-knack*). You can't sell this, for God's sake.

ANGEL. The other one, the niece, I think she's in Reception.

SVETAN (*angry*). You're crazy, going to the dump after hours! You'll get us into trouble, they've complained –

ANGEL. Hoover doesn't like her working in the bar –

SVETAN (*cutting in, angrier still*). People wrote to the papers –
you read it out to us! That man from the council – he told
the Captain we had to get permission to go to the dump;
and never at night – absolutely not allowed –

ANGEL. It's not dark at night here – not at all.

SVETAN. It's like a swamp, after all that rain.

ANGEL. You know what Shetlanders call these nights?

SVETAN. You'll sink in that shit.

ANGEL. The Simmer dim.

SVETAN. You'll drown!

ANGEL. The Simmer Dim . . . You should learn English,
Svetan, while we're here. We may not be sailing for a long
time yet. We should meet some nice girls. (*Searches
through his junk.*) See – this motor – it's from a washing
machine. I can mend that, I can use that for something. And
the paint – look – three tins, never even opened. I can get a
painting job round Lerwick – a fence, or a shed . . . .

SVETAN (*not interested*). What colour?

ANGEL. Fuschia. Mama's favourite. Which girl do you like?

SVETAN. What the hell does it matter? We can't go over to
the pub, we haven't any dough. We can't ask them on
board! What did you ask them on board for? We've no
coffee. No sugar. No soap left to wash with. No decent
shirts to wear.

He kicks at a piece of ANGEL*'s junk.*

ANGEL. Hey, hey.

Retrieves it.

SVETAN. The Captain's still in his cabin.

ANGEL. He didn't go to the shipping agents?

SVETAN. Went first thing.

ANGEL. Did he get them to phone the company?

SVETAN. Won't say. Been shut in his cabin ever since. He's sick. He says.

A pause. Suddenly ANGEL *thumps his belly quite violently.*

ANGEL (*to his belly*). Belt up, d'you hear? Damn belly, you sound like a whale. You think I don't know how hungry you are?

ANGEL *picks up some of his junk, is going to take it on board.*

I could eat a horse.

SVETAN *isn't really listening. He's looking over at the hotel, hoping for a glimpse of* MENA, *or just thinking about her.*

ANGEL. I could eat a camel . . . I could have made a few levi, selling on that bike . . . What's for supper?

SVETAN *is only half-listening.*

SVETAN AND ANGEL (*both absently, not to each other*). Fish.

SVETAN *walks/wanders into next scene.*

Scene Two

Hotel (reception).

SVETAN *is hanging around.* MENA *enters with a tray (trolley?) of coffee cups and stuff. She barely looks up at first, merely notices that a customer is there. She's busy manoeuvring trolley, or tray (remnants of dining-room desserts and coffees).*

MENA. The dining-room's closed. You can still get a meal in the bar – down that passage, on your left. Actually it's just as quick to go outside, and in by the street door, it's round the corner, opposite the harbour. (*Recognising him,*

acknowledging it shyly.) But you must know the way – the
Ludmilla's been here months now . . .

SVETAN. What do I do now? She thinks I came here for a
drink. Or a meal!

Pause.

MENA. You don't speak any English?

He shakes his head.

Russian?

SVETAN. I'm damned if I'll speak Russian!

MENA. I don't know why I asked you that! It's not as if I
speak any –

SVETAN. What's she doing learning Russian?!

MENA. – don't speak anything at all – except English.

SVETAN. She learns Russian! From sailors?!

MENA. I'm not English, mind – I'm a Shetlander! Me and Brit
are the only locals working in the hotel – and my uncle of
course, he owns it. The chef's New Zealand, working his
way round the world. Kiwis always stop here longer than
they plan – something to do with the weather – it stuns
them! Chef says he's –

SVETAN. Svetan. Svetan Kralev.

MENA. I don't understand.

SVETAN. Svetan.

MENA. Mena. Philomena Jameson.

SVETAN. She meets sailors all the time.

MENA. A girl in every port, I'll bet.

SVETAN. Hundreds of them, all the time.

*She's pouring him coffee, offers it. He shakes his head, pats
his pockets in explanation.*

MENA. On the house.

*He sips. She thinks to offer the sugar – at his nod she
spoons sugar once, twice, then a third time into his cup.
Hands him a spoon. He stirs. Sip by sip, he concentrates on
every drop, then drains the dregs. She offers him more (or
dessert), he refuses (from pride).*

SVETAN. I wish – I wish we were somewhere else right now,
the two of us. Some place. One language.

MENA. I can feel myself blushing, which is stupid, so stupid.
Mena, you're making a fool of yourself.

She smiles, almost laughs.

(*To* SVETAN.) They need an extra hand in the kitchen.

He understands she's busy, has to go.

SVETAN (*strong Bulgarian accent – the phrase sounds
foreign*). Catchyoulater.

MENA. ?

SVETAN. I . . . catchyoulater.

MENA. Catch you later! Yes. Okay. Goodbye!

She turns and goes, saying briskly to herself:

A fool of yourself, Mena! A complete and utter fool of
yourself . . .

As she goes, SVETAN *turns to go too. He does so with
some outward sign of exuberance, leaping onto the
gangplank acrobatically or something . . .*

ANGEL *is (still) on deck restoring some of his junk.*

ANGEL (*to* SVETAN). Where you been?

SVETAN. English lesson.

ANGEL. 'Bout time. Monoglot.

SVETAN *goes – below deck or off along the quayside.*

Scene Three

HOOVER *comes on. He is laden with as many bottles and packages as his carrier-bags, jacket, and poacher's pockets will carry.*

HOOVER (*shouting*). Ludmilla – ahoy!

ANGEL *appears on deck.*

ANGEL. Hoover!

HOOVER. Angel!

They continue talking as HOOVER *climbs the gangway.*

ANGEL. Hoover! Where have you been?

HOOVER. Ullapool. The place is as busy as Lerrick these days! Bung full: Poles, Russkies, Latvians, Africans – ! You know how many excisemen they have there now – sixteen! Tripping over each other up and down the pier. No chance for the wicked, none at all.

Both thump each other in greeting, like bears.

Here! Your favourite!

He shoves a huge tin at ANGEL.

ANGEL (*delighted*). Shortbread?

He opens it, eats some.

HOOVER. I thought I must have missed you.

ANGEL. Oh, we'll be here a long time, Hoover. A long, long time.

HOOVER. I thought you'd have sailed by now. The Sophia left Ullapool a couple of days ago.

ANGEL. They've sold her then!

HOOVER. Either that or the debts have been paid. One night she's in Loch Broom, under arrest – the next morning – over the horizon! So I thought you lot must have gone too.

ANGEL. No. The Ludmilla is still under arrest. 'By order of the Sheriff of Aberdeen.'

HOOVER. So – Samokov can't have cleared *all* its debts, then. Just enough to free The Sophia.

ANGEL (*shrugs, knows nothing of company details*). The Sophia is a lucky ship to be sailing.

Whilst talking HOOVER *unburdens himself of bottles and packages, sets them out on the table.*

HOOVER. Your mate Ganchov, he'd asked me to get hold of half a dozen babybuggies and a crate of aftershave. Still, I managed to shift them before I left. There's 50, 60 vessels in Ullapool right now, and more of them offshore. They're all needing buggies, aftershave, fridges, videos . . . .

ANGEL. Yes, Ganchov is lucky to go home.

HOOVER. The postie was the only one to wave them goodbye – he saw them before breakfast, piling onto the bus –

ANGEL. A bus! Oh, no. NO!

HOOVER. The replacement crew must have been slipped on board the night before. Sailed at dawn.

ANGEL. A bus! So Ganchov's flying back to Burgas! What about the Ladas? Gancha had Ladas on board The Sophia.

HOOVER. Maybe he sold them.

ANGEL. We need those Ladas, Ganchov and me. Now someone steals them. Oh, no!

He sits hugging the tin of shortbread, or eats some more of it.

HOOVER. He'll get them eventually – when the ship docks at Burgas.

ANGEL. Burgas! Maybe she goes to Falklands first, maybe Africa. Goodbye Ladas.

HOOVER. Ganchov's no fool. He'll sort it out. This sort of thing must happen all the time.

ANGEL. Yes. All the time.

HOOVER. Where is everybody?

ANGEL. Only skeleton crew left. You know why they call us skeleton? Because soon we will be.

HOOVER. Man, you'll never starve in Lerrick! Where's my good friend Barov?

ANGEL. The Captain is sick.

HOOVER. Sick?

He plonks a bottle down.

Tell him Hoover says come and take his medicine like a man.

ANGEL. Very sick.

HOOVER. Really? What does the doc say?

ANGEL. No doc. He flies home with the crew.

HOOVER. Bloody hell, what is this – the Marie Celeste?

ANGEL. Only skeletons left, Hoover.

HOOVER. You've been here months already – when was it, March?

ANGEL. Crew with wives and children go home. The Captain stays. I stay. And Svetan stays.

HOOVER. Svetan?

ANGEL. He was third engineer on the Kristina. The Company promote him – second engineer on Ludmilla. First time he comes to Lerwick.

NATKA *has come on with a bucket of water and a mop.*

HOOVER. Just the three of you?

ANGEL. Just the three of us.

NATKA *plonks down the bucket with deliberate clatter.*

ANGEL (*ignoring her, as if she hadn't entered*). – and Natka.

But HOOVER *has already seen her –*

HOOVER. Nadeshda! You stayed! I knew you couldn't leave me!

ANGEL. Because she speaks English, that's why she stays.

NATKA. Because she works like ten men, that's why she stays.

HOOVER. Natka, give us a kiss!

She swabs the deck.

When are you going to name the day? Ah, name it, Natka! They do a nice little wedding up at the Mission. Couple of hymns at the piano, tea and buns – back here for the whisky.

NATKA. Whisky?

ANGEL. Go get glasses, Natka.

NATKA. You got whisky, Hoover?

HOOVER. Everything, my heart's desire.

NATKA. Everything, uhuh – and whisky?

ANGEL. Glasses, Natka!

NATKA. Works like ten men!

She goes.

HOOVER (*to* ANGEL, *holding up a bottle of vodka to the light*). Look – don't you love this stuff? Look, look at that colour.

ANGEL (*still anxious about the Ladas*). Bloody wonderful, yes.

HOOVER. I can never make it out. Is it really green, – or is it just the blade of grass in there makes it look green? . . . Does it look green to you?

ANGEL (*making the best of things*). Hoover, we keep drinking it – one day we find out. Natka!!

HOOVER. I had a great time in Ullapool. Bloody wonderful! Some Polish celebration or other. Or it might have been a Scottish one. Can't remember. Sold aftershave like it was Christmas. Videos, whisky. Shifted the lot. Plenty more where that came from though, just say the word.

ANGEL. Hoover: no money.

HOOVER. Man, you'll put me out of business. What about half-a-dozen babybuggies – at a knock-down price?

ANGEL. If things get worse I will have to sell the Ladas.

HOOVER. I thought they were on their way to the Falklands.

ANGEL. *My* Ladas, my own – I have two here on the Ludmilla.

NATKA *brings food, forestalling Lada talk for the moment – spreads it out as if it were a feast – it is, it's all they've got left. Plus glasses for the spirits and the chasers. (Also they all smoke – HOOVER's generous with the cigarettes.)*

HOOVER. Wonderful, Natka. Wonderful spread. What's this – here, you shouldn't open this, I brought this for you lot. Keep the pâté and stuff for later. I'm not –

ANGEL. Sit!

NATKA. Eat!

NATKA *still arranging stuff on the table.*

HOOVER (*protesting*). No, no this'll never do. I've already eaten, I brought this for –

ANGEL. Eat!

NATKA. Sit!

HOOVER (*giving up*). Two Ladas on the Ludmilla, you say?

ANGEL. Three – but one is Minko's.

HOOVER. If they sell the ship, how do you get them home?

ANGEL *shakes his head, groans, miserable.*

HOOVER. Maybe you should sell them to the Poles.

ANGEL. We bought them from the Poles. Minko and Ganchov and me, we will have taxis. Like you Hoover. Land taxis first, and later sea taxis also. Then we will get rich, and I will build my house.

HOOVER. The house at Golden Sands! (*He toasts.*) To the villa Angelova at Golden Sands!

They drink to Golden Sands. They throw the shots of vodka down at a gulp.

NATKA (*with approval*). Hoover: you drink like a Bulgarian!

HOOVER. Practice makes perfect.

NATKA. A lot of these Western guys, they sip, sip – like it was tea. Or gulp, like it was water. Then they fall over. This is not acceptable in Bulgaria. Only Romanies and Poles fall over drunk. To drink, to really drink, you also must eat.

HOOVER. My grandad drank vodka with the early Klondykers. In the sixties. Russkies, they were.

NATKA. Rooskies, huh!

HOOVER. Klondykers weren't allowed ashore in those days. We were bloated capitalists! But now and then a dinghy would slip into some peerie voe, where there was no-one to fuss. My da found three Russkies once, down on the banks, trying to catch one of his Shetland ponies. They couldn't believe their eyes –

SVETAN *has come in.*

HOOVER. Hello there, lad.

ANGEL. This is Svetan.

HOOVER. I'm Hoover.

They shake hands.

ANGEL. First time in Lerwick.

HOOVER (*filling a glass, handing it to* SVETAN). Svetan! Welcome to Lerrick!

NATKA (*to* HOOVER). So the Rooskies tried to steal your pony?

HOOVER. Not at all, not at all. They wanted to check it out, that's all. A horse that small – they thought it must be a toy – a fairy maybe! So – one thing led to another – by which I mean – a dram or two! Next night they brought the vodka. Kept in touch for years after that. Once they sent my sister a fur hat. Oh, a beautiful thing – beaver, it was. She never wore it, just kept it in the press. When Mena was a peerie lass she'd ask to take it out, she'd nuzzle it and clap it, like it was alive!

SVETAN (*to either* ANGEL *or* NATKA). 'Mena'. Is he speaking about the girl?

HOOVER. She wears it sometimes now. When our Philomena wears that hat she looks – like someone else. Exotic.

SVETAN. What does he say about Mena?

ANGEL's and NATKA's *attention is elsewhere – with the food and drink and/or* HOOVER's *story.*

HOOVER. Not that Mena isn't a very pretty girl. She is – a bonny, bonny lass. But she's a Shetlander, she looks right Shetland. Till she wears yon hat. Then she's Russian – or Bulgarian.

But HOOVER *notices* NATKA *and* ANGEL's *reaction to this last statement.*

SVETAN. What does he say about Mena?

But they ignore him.

HOOVER. Of course, I know Russia isn't the same. Russia and Bulgaria – well, that's like Shetland and Scotland.

ANGEL. No. Not like Shetland and Scotland.

NATKA (*to* ANGEL, *in Bulgarian*). He hasn't a clue!

ANGEL (*pressing food on* HOOVER). Eat! Enjoy! (*To* NATKA, *in Bulgarian.*) Of course not – how can he?

HOOVER. No, no – I brought the salmon for you lot.

NATKA. Eat!

HOOVER. No, lass, this won't do at all.

But even as he speaks, he has to give in, as food is piled on, around his plate.

It's not like the Captain to miss a party. We'll get a Lerrick doctor to him.

ANGEL *shakes his head.*

HOOVER. Fair dos. Fair dos. Your ship's dentist made me a grand set of teeth – now it's my turn – I'll get Doc Bain –

ANGEL. No use. Very kind, but no use.

NATKA. The Captain has cold feet.

HOOVER. Cold feet?

ANGEL. A good man –

HOOVER. – sure, the best –

ANGEL. But his feet are cold.

NATKA. He phones the Company to ask for our pay. We haven't had any, not for a long time. No pay, no bonus. And now, no supplies even: no work clothes, no boots, no medicine, no food.

HOOVER stares at his laden plate of food in silence, pushes it away. NATKA pushes it back – she doesn't see the connection with the conversation and the hospitality.

NATKA. Eat. Eat.

HOOVER. So what did they say – to the Captain?

NATKA (*shrugs*). The Captain comes back, says he's sick, goes to his cabin, locks the door.

HOOVER. They gave him a bollocking, then.

NATKA. Or a deal.

HOOVER. What kind of deal?

A long pause. The Bulgarians don't discuss current events/politics easily.

ANGEL. Maybe he gets sick; gets plane ticket, goes home; gets bonus, or new job, new ship. With the same company, or another company. All companies in Bulgaria – (*Makes a twisting gesture.*) tied together – with each other – with the government.

Then he has a feeling he has said too much.

NATKA. Maybe we don't talk about this right now.

ANGEL. No.

SVETAN (*who is letting this dialogue wash over him*). Skol!

They toast and drink with him.

ANGEL. Tomorrow we unload the fish.

HOOVER. What, the three of you?

NATKA. We hire a fork-lift, and a driver.

HOOVER. At least there'll be some money for you when the work's done.

NATKA. You think!

HOOVER. Don't shift it then.

ANGEL. Then someone else shifts it.

HOOVER. No-one here'll shift it. We've got unions here in Lerrick, Angel.

ANGEL. We've got families in Burgas, Hoover. Even skeletons with no wives, they have family at home.

NATKA. And if we say 'no, we won't unload the fish', how do we get home? Swim?

HOOVER. Hell, nobody can stop you from –

ANGEL. When the Company send the plane tickets: then we can go. Only then.

SVETAN (*to* NATKA, *Bulgarian*). The visitor isn't eating. Maybe he doesn't like it – we should find him something else.

NATKA (*to* SVETAN, *Bulgarian*). The larder's empty.

HOOVER (*to* ANGEL). Man, you've had a revolution!

SVETAN (*to* NATKA, *Bulgarian, doesn't matter if we can't hear,* HOOVER *talking on over this*). Don't we have cheese still? Gherkins?

NATKA (*to* SVETAN, *Bulgarian*). No cheese. No gherkins.

HOOVER (*to* ANGEL; *in over* NATKA*'s last phrase*). I know it was only a few months back – but things are changing – aren't they? That's what revolution's for!

ANGEL. Remember when the Rooskies had their coup? When Yeltsin stopped the tanks? For 'democracy'! Well, the next day we went over to the Suloy. Remember her?

NATKA. Rooskie bucket!

ANGEL. She was anchored off Bressay. The Suloy crew had promised us new videos, we were sick of our old videos. So we take the dinghy. Wind, rain, bloody hell, waves up, down, up, down. But when we get to the Suloy there's someone high up on the funnel; he's unscrewing the hammer and sickle from the funnel. I say to the Rooskies: tell that guy watch out – wait till our dinghy's clear. If that lump of metal hits us – boom – we go with it to the bottom of the sea. And one of the Rooskies, he says: You think we're crazy? You think we throw this in the sea? So today Moscow radios: 'Take down hammer and sickle, destroy immediately.' But what do we know? Maybe Friday, maybe next month, maybe three months' time – Moscow radios again: 'Put back hammer and sickle. Immediately.' And where would we be?

NATKA. At the bottom of the sea. (*Laughs.*)

ANGEL. You wouldn't laugh like that in Burgas.

NATKA. We're not in Burgas.

Scene Four

ANGEL, MENA.

ANGEL *is phoning from hotel reception.* MENA *is also there – on duty (sort of), but not busy.*

ANGEL. Hello? Hello? Mama? It's your little Angel here. It's me, Angel. How are you, are you well? ARE YOU WELL? No, ANGEL! Fetch Aunt Evgenia – EVGENIA – . . . Remember not to shut the apartment door – you'll lock yourself out again. Then where will we be . . . Hurry, hurry, Auntie, it costs, waiting costs, walking so slowly across the hallway costs . . . Aunt Geni – hello. Yes, I'm okay. And you? And Mama? . . . (*Shrug.*) Who knows? Maybe we sail again, maybe they sell the ship, maybe they fly us home. Nobody knows . . . Yes, I have the catalogue, lots of dresses for you to copy, lots of pages. Kay's catalogue – very big . . . Coats? Sure, there are coats . . .

No, I can't buy any coats, Aunt Geni . . . I know summer
doesn't last forever, I know . . . size 18, I know, I know, not
green, or brown, yes – but listen – Geni – listen . . . . . Yes,
I know how you and Mama like them, big pleat at the back,
wide sleeves, yes, yes – but listen – look, it's important –
listen, look – Are you getting the money okay? Is the
Company paying the home allowance? Is it still being sent
to Mama? . . . No, of course they'll go on paying, always.
Just checking, Geni, just checking. Don't worry, they have
to pay the home allowance. Always. Always. But we
haven't any bonus – not for a long time now, and now no
wages, none at all. So no coats this year. Not even Oxfam
coats, no – but look . . . Geni, listen . . . Hello? – Hello
again. Have you heard any rumours round the port? About
the Company? Has Ganchov been to see you? Go and see
Ganchov, will you? Go and see his wife, she works in the
office, she'll know – Hello? . . . Hello? . . .

No answer. He bangs/throws down the phone.

MENA (*busy in reception . . . or not busy in reception*). I'm
not surprised the phones don't work in Bulgaria.

ANGEL. Telephone cards! The mission gave us these on
Sunday. Finished after one minute! (*He throws the card
away in disgust.*)

MENA. Maybe you got cut off. (*She picks the card up and
hands it to him.*) Try it again. Best make sure it's all used up
before you throw it away.

ANGEL. I can't call them now. They'll be almost back in the
kitchen by now.

MENA. ?

ANGEL. It takes them so long to get to the phone.

MENA (*politely*). You must have a big house.

ANGEL. Sure. It's big. Very big house.

MENA. You can phone from the office anytime. Hoover won't
mind.

ANGEL. You are very kind . . . You should be my girl.

MENA. I beg your pardon?

ANGEL. A girl like you. Too pretty for Svetan.

MENA. Did Svetan say I was his girl?

ANGEL. You're not Svetan's girl?

MENA. That's none of your business . . . Did Svetan – Who said – Did someone say – ?

ANGEL. You *are* Svetan's girl, then!

> ANGEL *clunks his head down on the reception desk, or hits his head hard with the flat of his hand, or something.*
> MENA *embarrassed. She picks up two large carrier bags from under/behind reception desk and walks out and along the quay.*

ANGEL. I saw you first . . . Sure, a big house. Very big. . . . 'The Burgas Land and Sea Taxi Company. Distance no object.' Soon I'll have the money saved. Build a house at Golden Sands. Video recorders upstairs, downstairs. Telephones all over, one for Mama, one for Geni. One for me and my girl. Blonde. Nice curves, strong legs. She watches while I push the children in the swing.

Scene Five

SVETAN *comes out on deck, sees* MENA. *(Quotes denote* SVETAN *trying out a phrase or word of English. The rest of the time each speaks his/her own language.)*

MENA. Svetan.

SVETAN. Mena.

MENA. Bonny weather.

SVETAN. Fine day.

MENA. I brought you these. From Hoover. Sausage; it's very good. Polish. And cake. The chef made that. Some oatcakes and stuff. And coffee.

She holds up big jar of instant. He starts down gangplank. He makes a gesture of thanks.

SVETAN. Coffee. Good. Now you can come and have some.

'Thank you! Come! Now!'

MENA. I have to go and get changed. I've just come off duty. I'm going out tonight.

SVETAN. 'Good. Come. Coffee.'

NATKA *has sloped on deck somewhere.*

NATKA. There isn't any coffee.

SVETAN *holds up the jar for her to see.*

SVETAN (*to* MENA). Why won't you come on board? You go on Russian ships. You talk to Russian sailors, you learn Russian with them. What's wrong with us?

NATKA. You talk too much. Anyway, it's all Greek to her!

SVETAN (*to* MENA). Look, we're not whiteslavers – Look, there's another woman on board!

NATKA *spits out her dog-end overboard, or something, looking really louche.*

MENA. I really must be going.

Almost as she says this SVETAN *holds out his hand to help* MENA *negotiate the gangplank, and as if her own words had meant the opposite, she takes his hand, and climbs aboard.*

SVETAN. Let's have some coffee, Natka.

NATKA. Natka's busy. Nadeshda 'really must be going'. (*Goes.*)

SVETAN *and* MENA *go below. He urges her to sit down.*

SVETAN*'s getting the coffee. (Or maybe neither of them remember about the coffee.)* MENA *is looking around the mess.*

SVETAN. This is where we eat. Galley. Television. Sit down, please sit down. (*He brushes a chair or bench.*) . . . You look as if you're just about to leave. You don't like it down here! Maybe you'd rather be on deck. (*He gestures, asking where they should take their coffee mugs.*) Here, or on deck? 'Up? Down?'

She doesn't understand.

'Okay? You okay?'

She nods. Goes to look out a porthole.

She's a good ship. You think she's a rust-bucket, I can tell. But that's not true. She doesn't deserve this. She needs paint; repairs. But – they pretend to pay us – so we pretend to work. But she's a fine vessel, really. 'Ship Okay . . . Ludmilla okay!'

She acknowledges the phrase, smiles. Looks about, or looks out of porthole. He's talking almost to himself now.

I never can explain about the sea. How I feel. Not to anyone on land – not even to – not even to people back home. But there's salt in your blood. You're a Shetlander.

MENA (*almost to herself*). There's salt in your blood. But I don't like the sea. I live on an island, but I'm no sailor. When I go to Aberdeen, I go by plane. (*Looks up at him.*) You wouldn't understand if I told you that.

SVETAN. The sea's in your eyes. All the colour of the sea: green, grey, black, blue –

MENA. Maybe you're making a fool of me? How would I know?! I can't stop listening to your voice – the sound of your language . . . Listen, I've got to go. Jesus, how did I get into this? It's crazy. *I'm* crazy. I have to go – I'm going out with the girls tonight – to the club – 'for a laugh'. And I'm not even changed –

SVETAN. We could go for a walk. And come back again for coffee. Or whisky, maybe there's some of Hoover's whisky left. 'Coffee? Whisky? Rakia?'

MENA. Svetan Kralev, I have to go!

SVETAN (*frustration makes him sound angry*). 'Okay? OKAY!'

MENA. You see the wynd, up there, leads up to the P.O.? Post Office? See the sign, further up – green and yellow lights – you can only see a bit of it.

SVETAN. Ah – 'Yellow Submarine!'

MENA. You know it? You've been out dancing at the Sub?

SVETAN. They bounced us out for not paying. But maybe they won't remember. I can bounce in without paying. Maybe.

MENA. The girls'll take the piss. I'll never live it down. (*To* SVETAN.) Nine o'clock.

She looks for her watch – she hasn't got it; she looks for his, he doesn't have one. She holds up nine fingers.

Nine! See?

SVETAN. 'Catchyoulater!'

MENA (*rushing off*). Jesus, this is crazy.

SVETAN (*calling after her*). 'Catch you later!'

MENA *turns straight into next scene.*

Scene Six

MENA, BRIT.

MENA *arrives, late.* BRIT *is already getting dressed, made-up, for a night at the 'Sub'.*

BRIT. A klondyker who doesn't clock a word you say?!

MENA (*starts to get ready for the evening also*). Who talks at the Submarine, anyway?

BRIT. Fair enough. You can't even hear the music – you feel it through your guts.

MENA. Afterwards is when you talk – walking home – saying goodnight . . .

BRIT. Are you serious?

Yes, she is.

You are. You're serious!

MENA. Well – when do you talk then? When do you talk?

BRIT. Get a bloody move on. (*Or merely signals this.*)

MENA. Twin room, double room, bed, breafast, dinner?
    Shower? Bath? It must have been a rough crossing, did you
    breakfast on the boat? New Zealand? Australia? And is this
    your first visit? Japan? Nova Scotia? Welcome to Shetland.
    The plane was late? Did you have a good flight? Trip?
    Evening? Day? Stay? Full Shetland breakfast? Coffee? Tea?
    Talk/talk/talk/talk . . . (*A couple more 'talk's if necessary.*)

BRIT (*on the final stages of 'getting ready'*). If you want to be
    late, it's up to you . . . Have you told Hoover yet? About us
    going walkabout?

MENA *shakes her head.*

BRIT. You are still saving up?

MENA (*over this, quickly – suspiciously quickly*). Sure.

BRIT. Tell him! You keep putting it off!

MENA. He brought me up!

BRIT. So?

MENA. Sometimes he feels bad about my Dad.

BRIT. It was an accident. If it was anyone's fault it was the
    Klondykers' – they shouldn't shout for sea-taxis in weather
    like that.

MENA. If Hoover had been there he'd have stopped the boat
    going out.

BRIT. He takes the boat out in all weathers himself. Anyway,
    he wasn't there – he was in Ullapool, or Aberdeen, or half
    way to Norway. He's never home for more than two
    minutes. Why should he mind you seeing a bit of the world?

MENA. He'd never leave Shetland, though.

BRIT. No-one's asking you to leave. Not for good.

MENA. Would you leave for good?

BRIT . . . Yes, I bloody would leave for good. My brother's left; half our own crowd have gone.

MENA. Some of them are back – Finn's back, he's opened a restaurant.

BRIT. Book a table quick then, it'll close in a week. Right, that's me. I'm off. See you at the Sub.

Calling back as she is almost off, or off.

And get a bloody move on!

MENA. . . . Maybe I'll leave. Maybe one day I'll leave for good . . . Don't want to leave.

Would he really tell the crew I was his girl? He's not the type to do that. Svetan Kralev . . . How do I know what type he is!

Scene Seven

ANGEL, NATKA.

ANGEL *tinkering, mending some piece of junk.* NATKA *comes on deck for a smoke, and a bit of air.*

NATKA. That chimney over there – over on the island – that's been burning night and day ever since we've been here. Never been out.

ANGEL *ignores this.*

NATKA. There's fires like that back home.

ANGEL. You from the mountains?

NATKA. Uhuh.

ANGEL. Long way from the sea, then.

NATKA. The sea runs in my veins too, Angel Angelov.

ANGEL. Not mine. No.

NATKA. What you doing here, then?

ANGEL. Mama wanted this for me. Marine college. Uniform. Money!

NATKA. Money?

That's a big laugh.

ANGEL. There was money then, before the 'coup' –

NATKA. Not for the fish-gutters!

ANGEL. – better than anyone got on shore. Much better.

NATKA. Ah, yes, when we were all comrades!

ANGEL. We're still comrades, aren't we? Democratic comrades.

NATKA. *Capitalist* comrades. Unpaid capitalist comrades. No dentist, no doctor, no medicines, no overalls, no boots, no gloves – who needs gloves, anyway, there's no fish to gut. Hardly any food – except for fish – hardly any rakia . . . even Hoover's whisky and vodka almost gone . . .

ANGEL. Go home, fishgirl. Get married in the mountains.

NATKA. The mountains! I'm not going back there!

ANGEL. Why not?

NATKA (*gestures towards the sea beyond*). That's why! That!

ANGEL *follows her gesture, glances perfunctorily out to sea.*

NATKA (*angry*). The sea! The goddam beautiful sea! . . .

ANGEL *ignores this, goes below.*

And I'm tied to this tub. And the tub's tied to this bloody rock!

She stays on deck during next scene.

Scene Eight

Blast of disco music (off) from The Yellow Submarine as people are exiting.

BRIT. Mena! Mena – come back – for Pete's sake – Mena!

> MENA *comes on, followed by* BRIT *(she carries her bottle of Becks, and* MENA*'s too).*

BRIT. What's up with you? Company not good enough for you?

MENA. I've had enough, that's all.

BRIT. So he stood you up – so what? Plenty more fish in the sea.

> SVETAN *steps out from where he's been waiting.*

> *He and* MENA *just stand staring at each other.*

So he didn't stand you up. Just took all bloody night to get here.

> SVETAN *and* MENA *just stand staring at each other.*

Or maybe he's been waiting outside all night. Maybe he couldn't get into the Sub. They've no money for the pub – so how would they have enough to get into –

MENA. Jesus! I'm an ejit, I never thought! Shit! If you've no money for coffee – how could you pay to get into the Sub?

SVETAN *(in Bulgarian).* Coffee? Finally she wants coffee.

MENA. Have you been waiting since nine? I never thought to come outside – I was too busy dancing. I didn't want you to come in and see me standing around waiting. For you. So I – Jesus, I'm sorry.

> *Impulsively she kisses him on one cheek.*

MENA. So sorry.

> *They are very close, staring at each other. They kiss again, quite chastely (oblivious of* BRIT*).*

BRIT (*to herself*). 1994? Is it?

SVETAN (*to* MENA). Yes. So sorry.

They kiss again.

BOTH. Sorry.

BRIT. 1894!

From The Yellow Submarine some music (off) starts up. The couple walk into the night. BRIT *loiters, takes a swig of her drink.*

NATKA *calls from the gang-plank.*

NATKA. You got a cigarette?

BRIT. Don't smoke . . . (*Offers* MENA*'s bottle.*) Want a drink? It's Mena's. Don't suppose she'll be back for it.

NATKA. Thanks. (*Not too impressed.*) Lager.

BRIT. Look, don't worry, I'll drink it, I just thought you might –

But NATKA *is draining the bottle, or most of it, slowly but without a pause. She hands the bottle back to* BRIT.

NATKA. Thanks.

NATKA *goes back to ship, or walks along the quay (off).*

BRIT *goes back to 'Submarine' (off).*

Scene Nine

MENA, HOOVER, BRIT.

The bar/reception.

An argy-bargy. HOOVER*'s been questioning her,* MENA *is indignant.*

MENA. You know who I was with! If you didn't see me, half Lerrick did – and the other half all know about it! . . . Anyway, he's nice, he's a really nice boy.

HOOVER. He's not a boy, Mena, he's a man –

MENA. I'm not a girl, either – I'm –

HOOVER. – Yes, you –

MENA. – eighteen –

HOOVER. – just.

> BRIT *comes in with trolley of either bedroom or dining-room stuff.*

MENA. I thought you really liked the Ludmilla crew –

HOOVER. I do. Always have.

BRIT (*low*). You drink with them hard enough.

HOOVER. But that boy –

BRIT (*low*). 'He's not a boy, Mena – he's a man – '

HOOVER. – he's new on board. I don't really know him.

BRIT (*low*). Meaning: 'he's far too fanciable'.

HOOVER. Hardly even talked to him.

MENA. He doesn't speak English.

HOOVER. Well, there you are.

MENA. Well, there I'm what? . . . What?

BRIT. For Crissake, Hoover, it was Friday night.

> She only wanted him for his body . . .
>
> *Silence.*
>
> Joke.
>
> *Silence.*

HOOVER. See and get the tables done before twelve.

> *He goes.*
>
> *Silence. The girls continue working.*

BRIT. Well . . . You must have had his body by now.

MENA. Don't be gross.

BRIT. Gross! You weren't back here to set up the breakfasts. *That's* gross!

MENA. We didn't notice the time. We were talking.

BRIT. Bulgarian?

MENA (*doesn't even hear this, dreaming of* SVETAN). I can't see him again till tomorrow. I'm on reception tonight. It was difficult explaining –

BRIT. It would be – in Bulgarian . . . That's the trouble with you Sunday School types – one or two nights down The Submarine –

MENA. What do you mean? I've been down the Sub countless –

We were talking – walking and talking.

BRIT. Well, you should bloody well have walked in here in time to do the breakfasts.

MENA. Please don't, Brit. Don't be angry.

BRIT. What really gets me is: you've been up all night, and you waltz in here, and you look – you look bloody fantastic.

MENA. Do I? . . . Maybe he'll be around this morning when I get my coffee break.

BRIT (*working away during this*). Well. Have fun. It's a holiday romance. Sort of. He's between jobs. So are you. Bev was showing me this handbook – lists of jobs, all over the world. The Aussies and Kiwis all swear by it . . . Do you fancy New Zealand? Actually, I don't think I do – too much like home – all those bloody sheep. California? Greece? Africa? . . . Mena, we ought to go soon – this autumn. Trouble is, Mum wants me to go on holiday with her first. She saw this coach-tour in the Shetland Times: 'From Hamavoe to Disneyland and back, 8 days.' Can you imagine – a bus full of ejits with helium balloons? And that's only the grandparents . . .

MENA *in a complete dwäm, folding the linen over and over.* BRIT *watches her a long moment.*

It's a holiday romance.

MENA *doesn't respond.*

Mena?

No response.

They could send another crew to replace them, any time. Tonight – tomorrow. Stick this lot on the next plane to Bulgaria. They could be selling the Ludmilla right this very minute in New York or Argentina. The crew would be the last to know. Or suddenly all the writs and fines are sorted, and she's away over the horizon before you can say P & O.

MENA (*hasn't heard any of this*). Brit – ? Are Bulgarians Muslims?

BRIT (*a beat; to herself*). Oo-oh, shit!

MENA. Brit?

BRIT. Get a bloody move on!

This next scene starts hard on BRIT*'s last words, maybe almost before* BRIT *has finished speaking.* BRIT – *and a moment or two later,* MENA – *move straight into this next scene; which starts instantly, cheerfully.*

Scene Ten

HOOVER*'s bar. The hooley. Everybody.*

Fiddle music. HOOVER *and* NATKA *dance onstage together. Whatever kind of dance it is – they dance wonderfully well together, with great style, and sexy humour.* (NATKA *is wearing a very odd, but quite exotic, outfit.*) *Cries and applause of appreciation from the others. They dance further off/offstage as* MANSON *calls for attention:*

MANSON. Ladies and gentlemen – a few words –

Some hubbub continues.

BRIT. QUIET – please! A few words from your President.

MANSON. A few words – as President of the North Lerwick Angling Club, I'd like –

BRIT *bangs on a tray to command attention.*

BRIT. QUIET – PLEASE! Or you'll be out on your arse!

MANSON. Thank you, Brit. Fellow anglers! A warm welcome to all – and especially to our guests from the Ludmilla. Tonight we've got some amazing entertainment – and some serious fundraising to attend to. Note the tombola over yonder. Chef made the cakes –

Boos and cheers.

Our good friend Angel here carved the ship

Cheers.

MANSON. Before the hooley gets under way, I have to introduce our newest LIFE member; who pit his wits today against the best anglers of Lerwick.

MENA. And the fish!!

HOOVER. And that's not all he's reeling in.

MANSON. A magnificent specimen, you'll all agree. Perfectly beautiful.

Hooches from BRIT. *But he means the fish – which is now handed to* SVETAN *for a photocall. He shakes* SVETAN'*s hand, freezes the handshake whilst someone (a couple of photoflashes) takes a photo of them and fish.*

SEVERAL (*during handshake and photo*). Speech Svetan. Speech Svetan. Speech Svetan. Speech.

Silence falls. And continues, as they wait for some words from him. SVETAN *beams, but doesn't know what to say.*

ANGEL. Say something. Just say it in Bulgarian.

MENA. Say something. Anything.

A pause. SVETAN *beams, holds up the fish. Just as he opens his mouth to say 'thank you', the fiddler,* HOOVER *and* NATKA *whirl into action.*

The others all hold up glasses; they and the dancers all cry:

Svetan/ Skol/ Svetan/ Skol/ Skol . . .

*

MANSON *and* ANGEL

ANGEL *is wearing seventies flares. He is lost in appraisal of his new tie.*

MANSON. That's quite a tie, Angel.

ANGEL *beams with pride.*

Used to have one very like it myself. Katie finally packed it off to Oxfam just the other week there.

ANGEL. You like this tie? Look, you take it, please –

He's already untying it. MANSON *stops him.*

MANSON. No, no, Angel – you keep it, I've plenty ties. Hundreds of them.

ANGEL. Sure?

MANSON. Sure.

ANGEL. Really sure? Look, I don't need –

MANSON (*coming in on this*). Quite sure. Wear it on Monday, when we meet with the other unions . . . Head Office had a fax today from your Embassy in London.

ANGEL. Embassies! They tell lies.

MANSON. Apparently Samokov claim you sabotaged their cargo.

ANGEL. The fish? No!

MANSON. But you refused to unload it yesterday – and again today?

ANGEL. Sure.

MANSON. So – you're on strike?

ANGEL. No, we do not strike. We do our job, we look after the ship, we look after the fish. The ship is worth nothing, she is old – but the fish! – The fish is worth money, lots of money.

MANSON. Samokov claim they can't pay you until they've sold the fish.

ANGEL. Do you believe this?

MANSON. It doesn't matter what I believe, Angel, as an argument it carries a certain –

ANGEL. We keep the fish. The fish is our strength. To bargain we must have strength, is that not so?

MANSON. The golden rule –

ANGEL (*cutting through this, ignoring it*). So long as the fish are on board, Samokov won't keep us short of fuel. The engines must run for the fish to stay frozen – and if the engines are running, we will stay warm.

MANSON. So – this is in fact a strike, then? An unofficial str-

ANGEL. We are not on strike. We absolutely do not strike. We look after the ship, and the fish. And we wait: for our pay; for the bonus; for the ship to be sold . . . or not sold; for the next job, or no job. We are not on strike. This is how we must live. All the time. At this moment we need the fish. This is not political. This is survival . . .

Someone fills up the glasses, or hands them a plate of eats. ANGEL *remembers this is a party; becomes more optimistic, confident:*

One reason why I stay as skeleton crew – I keep watch on my Ladas. Soon we will give up the sea, Ganchov and I, we will be rich. Like Hoover. 'Burgas Land and Sea Taxi Company. Distance no object'.

*

HOOVER, SVETAN . . . *and* BRIT *and* MENA.

HOOVER (*to* SVETAN). Learning the lingo?

SVETAN *doesn't understand. They both salute and drink.*

(*More to himself than* SVETAN.) Shouldn't be much of a problem – not with Mena teaching you. (*To* SVETAN *now, trying to make himself understood.*) I'm Mena's uncle. Well, you know that by now . . .

SVETAN *nods politely, without understanding.*

Me and Mena's da, we ran the taxis together. Sea taxis mainly: twenty minutes maximum from Lerrick to ship, or the agents dock the fee. I loved all that – still do – tearing through the waves, hailing the ship . . . Peter was more of a dreamer. Miles away, half the time. First he fell in love with my sister, then it was wedded bliss, then the bairn was on the way – more dreams, more plans . . . !

SVETAN *pours the remains of his beer can into* HOOVER*'s glass.* HOOVER *doesn't even notice.*

He fell between the ship and the boat. He got a call from a reefer – East German. I was at a wedding in Ullapool. The weather wasn't bad, not really. The winch slipped, he was knocked overboard. Between the ship and the boat . . .

Someone told my sister. (I was still dancing at the wedding, in Ullapool.) She went into labour. Mena was born early, a peerie, peerie babby. Aye, but it was her mother that died. My sister died.

SVETAN *uncertain how to respond, only knows it sounds serious.* HOOVER *notices there's some beer in his own glass (or the can) and pours it into* SVETAN*'s.*

I never talk about it. Everyone knows what happened. Except, that's not true – no-one knows what happened . . . The translator never got any sense from the crew. Koreans. Poor as mice, and scared witless . . . Sometimes I think I should talk about it to Mena. Sometimes I think she wants me to . . . But I wouldn't know how.

After a moment, BRIT *comes in, calling.*

BRIT. Hoover! Come and dance!

He doesn't respond. She approaches.

Hoover?

She wonders what is wrong, but SVETAN*'s no help.*

(*More quietly.*) They're asking for you Hoover. Everyone's asking for you.

After a moment he briskly slaps his hands on his knees, or claps them together, and gets to his feet.

HOOVER. Right, then. Lead me to it, girl!

BRIT *and* HOOVER *go.* SVETAN *remains. A pause.*

SVETAN (*in Bulgarian*). Christ, I'm knackered! (*Drinks.*) . . . I wish I could *say* something. (*Drinks.*) . . . I wish they wouldn't say so *much!* . . . Talk, talk, talk, talk . . . (*Drinks.*)

MENA *comes in. She signals to* SVETAN – *with a sign, or a gesture, no words – to come and drink/dance/ . . .*

A beat. Then he replicates HOOVER*'s response – the hands slapped on the knees as he rises.*

SVETAN. Right, then. Lead me to it, girl! (*He could be talking Bulgarian here, or could be approximating phonetically what he heard* HOOVER *say a moment ago – 'right, theyleame girl!').*

They go off together, not necessarily offstage.

*

NATKA, BRIT.

BRIT. Natka, what you drinking?

NATKA. Always finish up with whisky. Keep the best till last.

BRIT. That's a very . . . interesting costume. I suppose it's your national costume?

NATKA. This? Oxfam! I always go there.

BRIT. Don't suppose you get much chance to dress up on the Ludmilla?

NATKA. Sure we have chances. What do you think? Only four, five girls. Plenty good times, plenty good fights. Anyone says they don't have no love affairs at sea tells big whopping bloody lies. You ever met Minko? Chief of Fish-Freeze?

BRIT. I think maybe once I had to throw him out the pub.

NATKA. Minko the Armenian. Back in Burgas now, with the rest of the crew. Minko always said I had a head like cement. He liked that in a woman. S'beautiful man. Like Bronson.

BRIT. Bronson?

NATKA. *Charles* Bronson.

BRIT. Oh, right, I see! An ugly bastard!

NATKA. Go away. Get out of here.

BRIT *goes.*

You shout 'Bloody Klondykers!', I hear!

*

NORRIE MANSON *and* HOOVER.

HOOVER. Bugger the F.O. It's got bugger all to do with the F.O.

MANSON. It's got a lot to do with the F.O. We can't negotiate without them.

HOOVER. Why should they work overtime – as dockers, which they are not –

MANSON (*coming in over the last sentence*). Samokov are about to sell the Ludmilla and clear the debt.

HOOVER. Great, they can pay the crew then! Not just the skeleton crew, but the others back in Burgas! Who's buying?

MANSON. Stara – a bigger concern, much bigger.

HOOVER. Bulgarian?

MANSON. Yes. That's the worry. It could turn out to be an umbrella company, or a subsidiary.

HOOVER. Mickey Mouse money, you mean?

MANSON. Creative accounting. Yes. It stinks. Especially if you're the crew. But the Foreign Office maintains this case shows 'democratic change' is taking place in Bulgaria.

HOOVER. And my name's Santa Claus.

MANSON. Never mind Santa – it's the unions our Government refuses to believe in. Governments believe in trade . . . How is trade with you, by the way?

HOOVER. Fine. Oh – you mean I could be blackballed by Samokov? So be it.

MANSON. Samokov want that fish – badly – now. What if they send in the heavies to move it?

HOOVER. No-one in Lerrick's going to –

MANSON. Lerrick? Who says they'll come from Lerrick? Burgas more like!

HOOVER. They can't do that! It isn't legal!

MANSON. Easy to turn a blind eye if it's already done. Of course they might have to remove the crew first –

HOOVER. They can't do that – !

SVETAN *comes in drowning* MANSON*'s last words.*

*

SVETAN (*drunk*). Talk, talk, talk, talk . . . Listen to me.
Everybody's making such a bloody noise. I'm making a
bloody noise. In Bulgarian.

*A quiet descends on the hooley. He's obviously demanding
attention. But the two who can understand him look serious
as he delivers the next paragraph, and are on the verge,
through it, of interrupting/stopping him.*

Nobody shouts in Bulgaria. Did you know that? We speak
very quietly in the bars and the cafés. My little girl, she's
four, she goes to nursery. Ssssh! Got to be careful what you
say. Kids talk to other kids, and other parents, and teachers.
Who knows what side they're on?

Well, now it's time to make a noise.

*As his voice rises again, the partygoers become less attentive,
though NATKA and ANGEL are still apprehensive.*

I'm sick of waiting and waiting for money and food and
soap and shirts and letters and phonecalls. I'm sick of
keeping quiet. Time to make a noise! We're going to get the
goddam fish. We'll go back to the Ludmilla – We'll wake up
the Captain –

MENA. What is he saying? What?

But they ignore her.

SVETAN. We're going to get the fish.

He climbs on a chair or table or something.

We'll get the goddam fish and we'll chuck it overboard –
chuck it in the harbour, every bloody box, let it rot, let it
stink –

MENA. What is he saying? Angel?

ANGEL. Nothing.

SVETAN. No – mustn't let it rot – I know – I know – we'll get
Hoover's taxi, we'll, we'll go round Lerwick, we'll leave a
box on every doorstep, like the British milkman. Frozen fish
for every fridge in Lerwick – Lerwick? – everywhere –
Unst, Yell, we'll go to Fetlar – we'll take the ferry –

He breaks off, stands motionless. A pause. Just as some of them go forward to help him down.

Mena? Shouldn't have said about Lea. Didn't mean to talk about Lea.

Silence. They all watch – then, as he sways, some of them (ANGEL, HOOVER, MANSON, FIDDLER) dive forward – just in time to scoop him up, and take him off.

NATKA *resumes drinking.*

MENA (*to* NATKA). Did he – ? I thought – ?

NATKA *ignores this.*

I thought . . . Did he say something about me . . . ?

NATKA (*not addressing* MENA). Easy to be brave in the bar, at night.

MENA *follows the others off, or watches them go.*

NATKA. Not so easy in the morning.

Scene Eleven

The gangway of the Ludmilla is half up. BRIT *enters.*

BRIT. Jesus, it stinks in here. Worse than a brewery.

MENA *enters.*

(*To* MENA.) We should get a bonus for clearing this up! No sign of Hoover! Sleeping it off! Give him a shout, Mena, go on, wake him up –

MENA *isn't responding, just stands there.*

– tell him he's wanted on the phone, tell him he's got a very important customer –

MENA (*devastated*). He has . . . A very important customer. He's with him now, in the dining room. A horrible customer. He's having breakfast. Coffee, not tea . . . They're going away. Today. He's going away.

BRIT. Begin again.

But MENA *can't.*

Don't bother. I get the drift . . .

MENA. You think I can't, I hardly know him, it's daft, I'm
daft, but I'm not, I want to go with him, I want him to stay.

BRIT. Mena, they come back – every year, like the herring.
Besides, you can phone, you can write –

MENA. In Bulgarian!

BRIT. Well, learn the bloody language.

MENA. I want him to stay.

BRIT. Don't be stupid!

MENA. They need more coffee.

MENA is leaving, making for the Ludmilla.

MENA. Coffee, not tea.

BRIT *goes (off) to see to coffee.*

MENA *goes to the Ludmilla.*

NATKA *appears on deck (washing to hang up or something);
she sees* MENA *coming.*

NATKA (*yelling to* SVETAN, *off*). Svetan! . . . Svetan!

*She bangs something noisily against the
funnel/rail/whatever.*

(*To* MENA.) No head for drink, your loverboy! A disgrace
to Bulgaria.

MENA. You're going away. The new Captain, he's arrived.
You're going away.

NATKA (*yelling*). Angel! Svetan!

SVETAN *appears during* MENA'*s following speech.*

MENA. The other crew – it's coming – on the plane this
morning – the Captain's here already. He's phoning for a
taxi now.

NATKA (*to* SVETAN). Looks like we're on our way.

SVETAN's *listening to* NATKA, *looking at* MENA.

SVETAN (*to* NATKA). With pay-cheque or without?

NATKA *shrugs. They both know the answer.*

MENA. He's booked Hoover's taxi to take you to the airport.

NATKA (*coming in over this*). The taxi's booked.

MENA (*coming in on some of this*). I can't come with you to the airport, the Captain said: No.

ANGEL *appears on deck.*

NATKA (*to* SVETAN). The Captain's calling the shots.

SVETAN. The Captain?

NATKA. Replacement Captain. Or – whatever he actually is.

SVETAN. We'd better tell Barov, then.

ANGEL. Barov's gone – His cabin's empty. He must have slipped ashore last night. Or this morning.

. . . What's up? We're going home?

SVETAN. Apparently.

ANGEL. Now?

NATKA. Taxi's booked.

No-one's thrilled – too many forebodings.

ANGEL. Barov must be telling them why we 'sabotaged' the fish!

SVETAN. Barov? He never opened his cabin door!

NATKA. If they want details, he'll have to give them details.

ANGEL. He was at the meeting with the Unions. He certainly heard us then.

NATKA. Thank God he didn't hear Svetan's speech last night!

SVETAN. What speech?

NATKA (*to* SVETAN). Say goodbye to your little schoolgirl. (*Calling down to* MENA.) Goodbye little girl, we're going home.

SVETAN. I'm not going anywhere. I'm not going anywhere – not until I get my money.

ANGEL. You won't get money sitting around here.

SVETAN. I won't get any back in Burgas, that's sure! (*To* NATKA.) Minko told you on the phone he's had zilch – not a levi. And no job, either.

ANGEL. Svetan – it's time to go –

MENA (*calling up*). Svetan?

SVETAN (*to* ANGEL *and* NATKA). And have all this start over again? And again? And again? No pay, no news, even before the food ran out it wasn't fit for rats –

ANGEL. Svetan – it's over –

SVETAN. I'm not going –

NATKA. There's thirty crew on their way from the airport, some of them secret police. What are you going to do – shoot them?

SVETAN. Not going.

NATKA. You're drunk.

ANGEL. Crazy drunk.

NATKA. They'll throw you in the hold and forget about you – if you're lucky.

SVETAN. They're not coming on board until they bring my pay.

NATKA. This isn't the time to fall in love!

SVETAN. It's got nothing to do with Mena. So what if it has got something to do with Mena?

MENA (*calling to* SVETAN). What are you saying? Svetan – what are you doing?

ANGEL (*to* SVETAN). Calm down, you're hungover, we've got to get our things, and go –

SVETAN (*over this*). You get your things and go. What are you going back to? You'll be worse off than Minko.

ANGEL. To bargain you must be strong. Maybe we weren't so –

SVETAN (*in over this*). We're as strong as we'll ever be. We've got the fish – that's all they want. They don't want the ship – they've let her rot till she's fit for the scrapyard. And we'll rot too – here or Burgas, what's the difference –

ANGEL. You don't even speak Engl –

SVETAN. Go! Hurry up and go! I'm pulling up the gangplank as soon as you've gone.

ANGEL *unsure what to do.*

NATKA *starts to light a cigarette.*

NATKA (*to* SVETAN). You can't stay on your own. You need someone to help guard that thing. (*Indicates gangway.*) You need someone to speak English.

SVETAN. Fuck. Off!

NATKA *is lighting a second cigarette from her first. He's about to refuse it.*

NATKA. Someone who works like ten men.

She hands him the second cigarette; takes up a position (beside him at the rail? at or on the gangway?), indicating that she is staying too.

ANGEL. Oh, no. No. Oh, Mama!

HOOVER *enters from pub. He has parcels, or carrier-bags, of goodies for them in his arms.*

HOOVER. Ludmilla! Ahoy!

He sees MENA *on the quay, clocks that* MENA*'s passed on the news.*

(*To crew*.) Captain Andronov is over at the agents'. He wants you ready for offski soon as he's back.

The three crew gather to the rail/gangway, but are silent. HOOVER *very aware of the tensions.*

HOOVER. The stand-in crew's on its way from the airport. I'm to drive you there now . . . Brought you these. (*The carrier bags.*) . . . Need any help?

ANGEL. We need a whole lot of help. Yes, Hoover, we need a whole lot of help. Because we have to stay here, on the ship. We are on strike. Yes, now we are really on strike.

Everything very still for a moment.

MENA. Are they staying? Svetan's staying? I've got to talk to him, I'm just going on board for a moment –

But the three crew are hurrying to pull up the gangway properly and make the ship secure.

MENA *wants to call out to* SVETAN, *but* HOOVER *restrains her.*

The three crew are still tying up, very thorough, or checking the finished operation, as the lights come down.

End of Act One.

ACT TWO

Scene One

SVETAN *lounges on bunk below deck with* MENA. *They've been in bed most of the afternoon.*

MENA. Tell me more. Go on. Tell me about Bulgaria.

SVETAN. In Bulgaria no rain. Hot sun – all the time, very hot. Black Sea very hot.

MENA (*correcting him*). The Black Sea *is* very hot.

SVETAN. The Black Sea is – (*Indicates some object which is blue.*)

MENA. Blue.

SVETAN. Black Sea very blue. I believe every sea hot, every sea blue. First time I go in ship – we go Murmansk! Baltic sea very cold. Very very cold like Shetland.

MENA. Shetland's not so cold really. It's – fresh.

SVETAN. It is wet.

MENA. Only for 280 days in the year. Allegedly . . . Do you find it very, very cold?

SVETAN. No. (*Meaning: not with you.*)

MENA. You're bound to find it strange – even people from Scotland find it strange.

SVETAN. The sheep is –

MENA. Are –

SVETAN. The sheeps are very small. The hedgehogs are very big.

MENA. Don't you have hedgehogs in Bulgaria?

SVETAN. Bears.

MENA. Bears?

It's so easy to wind her up. He speaks in careful, careful English.

SVETAN. In Bulgaria The Bears Are Blue.

MENA. Tell me something real, tell me something true.

But he's silent.

Tell me about Burgas.

SVETAN. It's okay.

MENA. Nessebur? Sunny Beach? Sunny Beach sounds nice –

SVETAN. No, not nice. This is beach for Party members.

MENA. Communists, you mean?

SVETAN. Sure.

MENA. Oh . . . Golden Sands? That's where Angel's going to build his house. Once he's got his taxi, and saved the money . . .

SVETAN. It's okay.

They fall silent. Bulgaria troubling SVETAN.

MENA. I do so love you.

But he says nothing.

Talk to me. Talk to me, like you used to.

Pause. She has moved in front of the porthole.

SVETAN. Come away! From the porthole – come!

She does so.

MENA. What do you think I'm going to do? Fall out?

SVETAN. Yesterday someone watch. On the quay.

MENA. Well, there's nothing odd about that.

SVETAN. Yes, odd.

MENA. It's the dead end of the harbour – people walk their dogs here, or pass on their way to the dump.

SVETAN. No. He watch Ludmilla.

MENA. Everyone in Shetland looks at the ships.

SVETAN. This person not Shetland.

MENA. How do you know?

SVETAN. I know.

MENA. Well, he wouldn't see much through a porthole . . . I ought to go soon. I'm on reception –

SVETAN (*sharply*). No.

MENA. I'm on reception tonight, I have to be –

SVETAN. When Angel and Natka come. Then I walk with you to Hoover's pub.

MENA. Because someone stares at your ship? What do you think he's going to do? Shoot you? . . . Shoot me?

SVETAN. Do not laugh upon this, Mena.

MENA. Svetan, we're in Shetland.

SVETAN. No, I am here on Ludmilla.

MENA. Don't be silly – you're in Lerwick.

SVETAN. Maybe he wants only make me nervous.

MENA. Who?

SVETAN. Maybe more – maybe hit my head – at night – no-one sees – I fall in harbour.

MENA. Brit was right – you've got cabin fever. Tomorrow it's Angel's turn to keep watch. We can go bowling, or dancing.

SVETAN. No.

MENA. Why not? Angel and Natka are in the pub right now.

SVETAN. They meet with unions.

MENA. Angel's always in the town.

SVETAN. To work: Paint house, mend telly, cut peat . . . Not now. No. Finish.

MENA. Not now? Because of the man on the quay?

SVETAN. Also yesterday Angel phone Captain.

MENA. Captain Barov?

SVETAN. Of course, Captain Barov. The other one was
Colonel.

MENA. No – you don't mean a colonel! A colonel can't be in
charge of a ship!

SVETAN (*ignoring this*). Poor Barov! No ship, no job, no
money, nothing.

MENA. He washed his hands of you lot! Locked himself in his
cabin! You said he must have been siding with the bosses –

SVETAN. They bite you anyhow. (*He mimes handcuffs.*)

MENA. The newspapers said he'd been up to something.

SVETAN. Bulgarian embassy tell this!

MENA. Black market stuff.

SVETAN. Black market! Philomena: black market is market.
Shops empty. All empty. We buy in street. Not shop. We
buy shoes, razorblades, coffee, sausage, soap . . . After ship
I go home, I sell radio, perfume, tampax, aspirin . . .

He's bitter, angry. She tries to calm him.

MENA. I know, I know.

SVETAN (*under her next words*). You don't know.

MENA. I know, I'm sorry. It's going to be okay.

SVETAN (*under her words*). No. Not okay.

MENA. On the local news last night they said there'd been
progress. The Shipping Minister said so. They've found a
buyer – this time it's for real – Japanese, I think . . .

SVETAN (*feels trapped; more to himself than her*). Someone
watch the ship.

MENA. I love you so much.

No response. She's exasperated, upset, near tears.

Listen, I'm talking to you – Look at me – Svetan, please –
there's a way out of this –

He turns away, or pulls away from her.

*Deeply hurt, she turns or backs away from him – and is
standing in front of the porthole again.*

SVETAN. Mena! . . . Come away! The porthole! Come away!

She picks up shoes, jersey, whatever, goes.

Scene Two

NATKA – ANGEL – BRIT . . .

The bar or reception of hotel. NATKA *helping out in some
way – cleaning, polishing, stacking glasses . . .*

NATKA *very angry. The fish-gutter is now on equal terms with
the engineers.*

NATKA. Of course she saw you! You steaming great hulk, how
could she NOT see you? She and her husband both saw you
the time before that, and the time before that, and the time
before that. DOPE! ARSE! Just thank the Holy Father you
picked a kind shopkeeper. Because you certainly couldn't
pay the fine. You could be in prison by now, do you know
that?

He mumbles something about prison being better than this.

No it wouldn't – Dope! It wouldn't be better than this. If we
ended up in jail, they'd just deport us back to Burgas. Or
some Shetlander would shame us by paying the fine . . .
Why do you have to steal? These people are never done
helping us. What did you pinch?

*He takes the items out of a poacher's pocket. She examines
the first of the two items:*

Hoover's got aftershave – cases of it. Dope! He'd have given you some. (*Examining second item.*) What do you want this for?

ANGEL. For my hair.

NATKA. *Carpet* shampoo?

But he's shambling off – passes BRIT *as she comes on, she wants to talk to him.*

BRIT. Angel.

He ignores or doesn't hear her.

NATKA (*calling to* ANGEL *over* BRIT'*s greeting to him*). You know what you are – a joke! A lousy, stupid – joke!

BRIT. Natka.

NATKA *shoves the carpet shampoo into* BRIT'*s hands/bosom. She clocks the label briefly.*

My favourite. Natka: about that stuff in the yard –

NATKA *looks or says 'don't know what you mean'.*

BRIT. These broken videos, and tellies –

NATKA. No, not me. Angel collects, not me.

BRIT. I don't bloody care who collects, but the stuff's all over the yard at the back.

NATKA. They get mended.

BRIT. They lie around out there for –

NATKA. They get sold, we get money. Shetland Times say – more than once – Bulgarians show good example, recycling.

BRIT. I couldn't get out the back door this morning! A washing machine – and that pushchair's been there for a couple of weeks! The brewery delivers at eight. If the fire officer saw that yard just once – .

NATKA. He mend *your* TV, Angel.

BRIT. So?

NATKA. So what you making a big noise for –

BRIT. Took me longer to get him out the bedroom than it took him to mend the thing.

NATKA. You have TV in your room?

BRIT. Well, it's Mena's too . . . Not that she's there much these days – nights!

NATKA (*bellows with laughter*). Ah, that little mouse, she can make some noise! I hear them both.

BRIT. You do?

NATKA. Snugasabuginarug. (*Another big laugh.*)

BRIT. Well, good for Miss Sunday School!

NATKA. Just like you and Angel, eh? Snugasabuginarug!

BRIT. No. Way.

NATKA. He says you're his girl.

BRIT. Medallion man! He's a joke!

NATKA. No. He is not a joke.

BRIT. You sounded pretty mad at him just now – whatever you were yelling in Bulgarian.

NATKA. Angel is not a joke.

BRIT. Did you see what colour he painted Norrie Manson's shed? Fuschia! Good thing Norrie's colour blind.

NATKA. Being here is not a joke.

BRIT. Look – I never said it was.

NATKA. We work, we don't beg. We wash windows, paint sheds, mend fences, cut peat.

BRIT. All I'm saying is –

NATKA. Angel is not a joke!

NATKA *walks off somewhere* (*not offstage*) *to phone.*

BRIT (*to herself*). All I'm saying is – one of these days –

NATKA *is dialling.*

BRIT *not in same 'space' now, wiping tables or something.*

BRIT (*to herself*). One of these days . . .

NATKA. Minko Borowski. Room 29 . . . Tell him it's Natka.
Tell him to hurry.

BRIT (*to herself*). . . . I'm going to break an ankle coming out
of that door.

BRIT *goes*

NATKA (*to herself*). Bloody phone cards! . . . Minko? . . . He-
e-e-ey! . . . Yes. Of course it's me. Sure, I'm okay. Sure I
miss you. How about you, Minko? Any redheads in Burgas
that can hold a candle to me? (*Great burst of laughter.*) Of
course you are – still better than Bronson. Well – still
younger than Bronson . . . Okay, Minko, cool your jets –
this is serious, – and the phone card's running out. Has the
company paid out yet? . . . But that's only a quarter of – . . .
What about the bonuses? . . . Bastards. Same for all the
crew? Jesus! What about work, have you got another ship
yet? . . . Have you tried the other companies – what about
Barowski? . . . None of them? . . .

HOOVER *in during next paragraph, deduces bad news
from her tone, stays very still, just lights up cigarette, listens.*

No, we've heard nothing – No, the post takes – No, we can't
use the radio any more, we need phone cards . . . Us? . . .
Here? . . . All three of us? . . . Just like the old days, eh,
same old routine! Could you go and see my sister? There's
no phone in those flats. Tell her – tell her don't take any shit
from the swine, it's nothing to do with her. Or the kids.

Watch yourself, Minko. Spit in their eyes for me – each and
every bastard. Watch out. Take care.

NATKA *goes and sits down. Absorbing the bad news.*
HOOVER *offers her a cigarette.*

NATKA. Captain Barov has been given a new ship – well, not
new, another one, bigger than the Ludmilla.

Minko's out of work – he told the newspapers about our strike. Now he's summoned to court – 'illegal activity'. He goes, he waits all day. They say, oh, the papers aren't ready; they send him away. Two weeks later they summon him again. Send him away again. And again. And again.

A pause. HOOVER*'s sympathy is silent.*

Svetan Kralev and Angel Angelov, engineers, and Natka Andonova, fish-girl, are all charged with treason.

HOOVER *half laughs/exclaims, it's so ridiculous.* NATKA *also.*

(*Serious.*) I'm scared . . . Yes, I'm scared.

Pause.

HOOVER. You married, Natka?

NATKA. No.

Pause.

Got kids, though. Two boys. Grown up now: fourteen, sixteen. They live with my sister. I teach them swim, I teach them chess, I pay food, clothes, rent. I'm a good mother, quite good. (*Pause.*) And I'm a very good father.

A silence. He gets out the cigarettes.

HOOVER. Might they put you in prison if you go back?

Silence. Maybe she nods a 'yes'. Both smoke.

You could help run the sea-taxi.

Pause.

It's not a ship, mind . . . .just a peerie boat!

They smoke. They don't look at one another.

NATKA. Boats are okay.

They smoke in silence.

Scene Three

SVETAN, MENA, BRIT. *On board Ludmilla.*

SVETAN. Political! Political! Always they say 'it is political'. No. No. I am not political.

BRIT. You're on strike. That's a political act.

SVETAN. I am not political.

MENA. It's just a word.

BRIT (*wryly*). Like 'revolution'.

SVETAN. I need my money; I am poor – not political.

BRIT. Just a word! Like 'poverty'! – just a word –

SVETAN. The unions say: fair day work, fair day pay. That is not political.

BRIT. – like 'coup', 'revolution', 'perestroika'? Just words? But they must mean something. What does it mean, Svetan, perestroika?

He shrugs, wants to drop it.

Come on, let's hear it straight from the horse's mouth.

SVETAN (*wants to give up*). I don't know horses.

MENA (*to* BRIT, *over this*). Don't be so mean. How can he explain, he hasn't enough English.

BRIT. Yes he has. Go on, what's it mean, Perestroika?

SVETAN (*asserting ignorance*). I sail far away. I am not in Bulgaria for very long time.

BRIT. Revolutions mean something. You must all have wanted something.

SVETAN. We want Bulgarian . . . Not Soviet. Bulgarian. We want read –

MENA (*corrects him*). To read. We want to read.

BRIT (*over this*). Sssh – shut up!

SVETAN. Read many books, newspapers . . . talk very loudly
in street, in café . . . buy tracksuit, buy Nike, be happy,
more money maybe . . . But also I want save –

BRIT. Save?

SVETAN. Yes, I want to save –

MENA (*correcting*). Safe. I want to *be* safe.

BRIT (*over this, to* MENA). Shut up. (*To* SVETAN.) So
Perestroika means safety. Right?

SVETAN. No. No. I want to be save like before.

MENA. Before?

BRIT. Under communism, you felt safe?

MENA. No, he doesn't mean that, he means –

SVETAN. Yes.

    MENA *dumbfounded.*

SVETAN. No.

MENA. So what does he mean?

SVETAN. Yes – and no. Like here. Sometimes no.

MENA. He thinks somebody's watching him here.

SVETAN. No, no. (*Meaning 'that is not what I'm on about.'*)
Like people here.

MENA. He thinks some secret police Colonel's coming to –

SVETAN. No!

MENA. Yes, you do, you may as well –

SVETAN (*impatient*). This is not what I talk. Before! Before
Perestroika. Always we have work, always (*Searches for the
word.*) apartment – always food. Always bread. Before.

MENA. And now?

SVETAN. Now my grandmother cannot buy bread. Three, four
times too much money.

BRIT (*drily*). And that's not political?

SVETAN. Peoples here also have no food, no work, no –
    (*Struggles again with the word.*) apartment. Sleep in streets.

MENA. But that's only – the homeless. You don't see anything
    like that in Lerwick.

SVETAN. Get killed in streets.

BRIT. Who?

MENA. Not by the police – For heaven's sake!

SVETAN. Black people.

MENA (*gently*). Svetan, not by the government.

SVETAN. They get you anytime! (*Gestures handcuffs.*)

MENA. Prison you mean?

SVETAN. I see on TV. (*Full flow.*) No work, no food, no
    apartment. Irish people, black people, old – old-clothes
    people (*Indicates ragged clothes.*) in streets, in prison,
    sometimes hurt, sometimes killed. One time killed inside
    police van.

The girls open their mouths, about to protest.

BRIT. No-one's saying that's okay –

MENA. At least it gets reported –

But his rush of words continues, angry.

I see on TV black lady – seek asylum – police fight her –
in apartment. She is killed in apartment by police. Like in
Bulgaria. Just like they kill my uncle in Bulgaria.

Silence.

BRIT (*very quietly*). Oh, shit.

BRIT *goes. Silence.*

MENA. Those things you saw on TV – I know they're bad, but
    it's not . . .

SVETAN. Shetland people very kind, Mena, I know this.

MENA. I suppose you're sorry you ever started the strike?

SVETAN. No, I am not sorry. I am completely, absolutely not sorry. I am proud. In Burgas the crew is very proud for us . . . But also I am angry . . . Also I am sad, too. As well.

MENA. I thought – I mean – you and me – we are –

SVETAN. I like it here very much. With you.

But he isn't looking at her.

MENA. Sometimes I forget how homesick you must be.

SVETAN. I want work, Mena. I want work – to work the sea . . . My other home – the sea.

Scene Four

HOOVER, MANSON, NATKA, ANGEL . . . *and* BRIT.

A meeting in HOOVER's *office (or the dining-room?)*
MANSON *not too happy about the information he has to pass on (as local union representative).*

NATKA. Files?

MANSON. Yes, Personal dossiers, files.

ANGEL. So what do we put in these files?

MANSON. Photo, qualifications, career details, and statements from you about everything to do with the Ludmilla Saga over the last year.

ANGEL. You think these files protect us?

MANSON. It's a precaution. We'll keep copies in Lerwick, we'll send copies to the T.U.C., to Brussels, to Sophia, and Burgas. Once the Bulgarian authorities know these files exist . . .

HOOVER. What? If the authorities know these files exist – what?

NATKA. We'll get our money, and work again on the ships, and everything is snugasabuginarug!

MANSON. The Bulgarian government has guaranteed Brussels
there'll be no victimisation of any crew member –

Everyone wants to say something, begins to say something –

– if you take this money, and these plane tickets, and go
home. On Tuesday.

Long silence.

ANGEL. The money is nothing.

MANSON. I know.

ANGEL. Not even a third.

NATKA. Secret police are like elephants – they never forget.
This year, next year, sometime . . . ? They can charge us
with anything – anytime!

MANSON. I know. However, I think we should set up the files
as soon as –

HOOVER. Is that the best we can do?

MANSON. Plus we're setting up a fund for phone and fax bills
for when you're back in Burgas. We'll make damn sure the
authorities know we're in contact. Very regular contact.

HOOVER. Jesus Christ, is that the best we –

MANSON (*getting louder, angrier towards the end of this
speech*). Yes, Hoover, it's the best we can do. Because our
own government won't talk to us, won't even listen to us,
just makes clucking noises. Because we're interrupting
Britain's plans to be the first into Bulgaria with the promise
of market forces, and what our government really wants is a
troop of Robert Maxwell lookalikes, talking banking and
business, and small, silly fish like us are nothing but a tiny –
but very very itchy – thorn in its side. Yes – it's the best we
can do – after months and months of committee meeting,
and negotiating, and phoning, and faxing –

BRIT *enters with sandwiches, tea.*

BRIT (*coming in on* MANSON's *words, as loud as* MANSON).
QUIET in there!

They stare. HOOVER *is angry.*

Keep it down a bit.

HOOVER. Who the hell do you –

BRIT. Keep it down – a lot. The Colonel's just been in.

HOOVER. What Colonel?

BRIT. The one who whisked Captain Barov away. Last
August? (*To* ANGEL.) It was you told me he's a Colonel –
right? – secret police? Well, he's back. Wants a room; single
with shower or bath.

HOOVER. We're fully booked.

BRIT. Yes, I know! Isn't it a shame? I told him to try the
Grand. But he hasn't left yet – he's ordered a brandy and a
coffee and he's sitting in the bar. By the window. You know
the corner window, where you can keep one eye on the
street, and the other on the quay? And if you've eyes in the
back of your head, you can keep an eye on reception too?

ANGEL. I think I go and help Chef in the kitchen for a while.
Natka?

NATKA. He won't come in here.

BRIT. No. But shouldn't you get back to the ship?

NATKA. Not yet. We don't want to meet the Colonel on the
quay.

BRIT. We'll come with you.

NATKA. *You* don't want to meet the Colonel on the quay –

HOOVER. Well, I don't know – I might enjoy –

BRIT. Svetan and Mena don't want to meet him on the quay.

NATKA (*to* MANSON). You must go and warn them, Mr.
Manson, on the Ludmilla – please.

BRIT *is going back to the bar, taking the tray.*

MANSON (*rising*). It is – just – possible the man's come to
negotiate a meeting.

NATKA. Sure – but what kind of meeting?

ANGEL (*going in direction of kitchen*). I go and help in the kitchen. I could eat a horse.

NATKA. Good idea, Angel. Plenty big knives in the kitchen.

MANSON, *on his way out, glances at her in alarm.*

NATKA. When I make a joke, I laugh.

A pause. Then HOOVER *slaps his hands on his thighs, or claps his hands together.*

HOOVER. Bugger the colonel! It's my birthday on Sunday. I'm twenty-one! Nadeshda, my heart's desire – you shall be my guest of honour!

NATKA. Maybe, maybe. But . . . will there be whisky?

HOOVER. Will there be – Look here, my lass, you cut me to the quick – the core – the heart. Have I ever denied you the water of life? And there's more! I will provide, for you (and other, inferior guests) mutton sandwiches, gherkins, Scotch broth, potato farls, mackerel pate, crabcakes, shortbread (for the minion Angel), macaroon bars – in short, a complete Shetland buffet. Ah, Nadeshda, Nadeshda, say yes. Make me a happy man.

NATKA. Okay.

HOOVER. Your place or mine? (*Down to earth now.*) Now – there's a daft question – it'll have to be the Ludmilla. With the gangway hauled up very very tight. I've a notion your Colonel's a skilled gatecrasher – but, hell, it's my birthday! – not the Secret Policeman's Ball.

NATKA. Okay. I will sing Happy Birthday To You. On the Ludmilla . . . If you want . . . .

HOOVER. I want, Nadeshda, I want! I want you to sing. I want you to dance.

He has got her to her feet. They stand, dancing-class style, in each others' arms, ready for the music.

I want you to forget about the fucking Colonel, and trip the light fantastic.

They are dancing now – beautifully – maybe with no music, just the dialogue in rhythm with the dance (or vice versa – have to work this out with the dancers!)

H. Have you thought any more about asylum?

N. Sure I think.

H. The job's still there

N. The seataxi!

H. Just the job for you, Nadeshda.

N. Work like ten men!

H. Five! Five! Work like five! I'll be satisfied with five!

HOOVER (*has her in some dance clinch*). When are you going to name the day?

They execute a spin turn/some nifty step. Stop.

Couple of hymns down at the mission?

She ignores this as she always has before.

Tea and buns?

They stop in mid-step, hold/freeze in position, eyes front.

NATKA. Whisky!

HOOVER. Whisky it is then! Marry me, Natka!

She's almost certain he's joking.

NATKA. Slavery? – Never!

HOOVER. Dammit, Natka – this is personal. I'm – (*Whatever age suits actor – old enough to be* MENA*'s uncle.*) I've got a nice little pub (the bank owns most of it, but I'm working on that); I've got a couple of taxis, one on land, one on sea – both in excellent nick – like me; I've got a niece who's like my daughter, I've got friends, neighbours, I love

eating, and drinking, and fishing and dancing. I love my
work. I'm a happy man. Marry me!

Long pause.

NATKA. For asylum? You ask me this for asylum?

Long pause.

HOOVER. Well . . . (*Long pause.*) . . . Sure – asylum. That –
goes without saying.

*He's about to say something, take her in his arms maybe
(but not so definitively that she understands his motives) –
but there are sounds from the bar and/or sounds of* BRIT
coming.

NATKA (*not hurriedly or furtively; maybe, from uncertainty,
trying to make light of it*). I tell you on Friday. When you're
twenty-one.

BRIT *comes in with the tray to collect the mugs, plates, or
trolley.*

BRIT. Colonel *Bogey* asked me to phone the Grand and see if
they'd a room – so I've booked him in there, good riddance!
But he hasn't gone yet, he's still through in the bar, he's just
ordered another brandy.

HOOVER. I'll do bar duty, then. As soon as he's gone, I'll
walk Natka and Angel to the ship.

BRIT. Mena's not back yet, I hope she tears herself away from
sailor-boy soon, the dining-room's filling up already.

HOOVER *goes.*

(*To* NATKA, *but busy with setting tables, loading trolley
with cruets, whatever.*) But at least that means we can refuse
the Colonel dinner!

Looks curiously at NATKA, *whilst loading tray, or
whatever.*

BRIT. You all right? The Colonel can't touch you in here. And
he can't storm the Ludmilla on his own.

NATKA. How old is Hoover?

BRIT. Don't know. But he could sort the Colonel if he has to.

NATKA. That wouldn't be a good idea.

BRIT. No?

NATKA. No. He never had a wife, then, Hoover?

BRIT. No! He's had plenty offers, mind – but he's too fly. His life's just about perfect as it is: wheeling and dealing, making money, losing it, and roaring around in that sea-taxi. My aunt set her cap at him once, but she kept baking him cakes – he can't stand the mumsy type.

NATKA. Hoover asks me to marry him.

BRIT. Bloody hell!

NATKA. You think I make a joke? When I make a joke I –

BRIT. No – No, no.

NATKA. You think Hoover makes a joke?

BRIT (*considers*). Hoover always means what he says. Even when he's joking. Even when he's drunk.

NATKA (*more to herself than to* BRIT; *coming to this conclusion*). It was for asylum.

BRIT. Oh, right – *You* asked *him* then?

NATKA (*stung*). No! Of course not . . . I think it was for asylum maybe.

BRIT. Do you want asylum?

Shrug.

You want to marry him?

NATKA *doesn't answer.*

BRIT (*as she is leaving, wonderingly, softly to herself*). Bloody hell!

BRIT *goes.*

NATKA. Silly cow! I don't want to marry him! . . . I want to live with him. Work and drink and dance and roar around the sea in his boat . . . With him.

As she sits there it grows darker. A faint buzz of noise (folk, or the bar telly, or both) can be heard now from the bar. NATKA rises, unhurriedly, and goes. As she does so, the COLONEL enters in the gloom. She doesn't notice him, he watches her go.

Scene Five

MENA *and the* COLONEL.

Hotel reception. Late at night. Shadowy light. Faint buzz of noise (telly in the bar?). MENA enters, busy clearing after dinners/setting tomorrow's breakfasts.

The COLONEL *stands, in the shadows, waiting.*

COLONEL. Good evening.

MENA barely looks, merely clocks that a customer is there.

MENA. The dining-room's closed.

She recognises him. Panics. Goes into automatic spiel.

You can still get a meal in the bar – down that passage, on your left. Actually, it's just as quick to go outside, and in by the street door, it's round the corner, opposite the harbour. (*Defiant.*) You know the way. You've been here before.

COLONEL. Miss Jameson? I have some information about your friends.

A pause. Then she makes for exit to bar.

Don't go.

She tries another exit route.

Please – don't go . . . The Company and our Embassy wish to convey their thanks for your help – and of course your uncle's. But – it's time to call a halt. We're all most appreciative. But – please, no more. These strikers don't need help, not now.

MENA. Yes, they do.

COLONEL. They're being well looked after now. Everything's under control. They have plenty money – plenty supplies.

MENA. No vitamins, no medicines, no food, no clothes –

COLONEL. Of course they have; they hide these things away. Goods like that – they're worth money back home. That's what this so-called 'strike' is all –

MENA (*bravely*). Why don't you pay them?

COLONEL. Because they're traitors. In our country, Miss Jameson, that's a serious offence.

MENA. It isn't true.

COLONEL. Your special friend, Kralev – the one you sleep with? In his cabin, on the Ludmilla? Most afternoons?

MENA. So?

COLONEL. Don't you know he lies?

MENA. I know he doesn't. He's a very honest –

COLONEL. Traitors put their friends in danger. Of course they never think of that. It's not important.

MENA. You're talking shit.

COLONEL. Quite right. It is – shit. Do you realise, Miss Jameson – it is Miss, isn't it, you yourself are honest in your life? – Do you realise that you, – or, at least, your uncle – is in danger?

MENA. My uncle? He's a Shetlander.

COLONEL. He shouldn't bite the hand that feeds him. The bigger the companies, the more they stick together. From Estonia to Korea. One word to the shipping agents and – (*Dusts his hands together.*) – Uncle Hoover will be a gentleman of leisure.

She's going to shout for BRIT *or chef* –

COLONEL. Don't shout – please! I do hate shouting. I feel obliged to put a stop to it . . . Nobody would know. Not even your foreign friend. The one you love? You're his passport, Miss Jameson, a piece of cardboard, nothing more.

MENA. I'm going to marry him, there's nothing you can –

COLONEL. What about his wife?

MENA (*a beat*). I'm going to be his wife.

COLONEL. And what about the kid? It's a girl. Do you think
your special, special Kralev would leave his kid behind?
In a country he says is so rotten he must leave it? But you
love him. You forgive him. You marry him. And then – ?
You live here together happy ever after in a little house in
Hamnavoe – and the rain beat, beating on the honeysuckle
round the door?

That is, if he stays. What do you think his game is? You go
to prison here for bigamy, I think? But by then he'd have his
passport. He'd be far, far away.

A silence. She can't answer this.

He hasn't even told you her name?

Straight into Scene Six.

As the COLONEL *disappears into the shadows, cut
immediately to* MENA's *scene with* SVETAN.

Scene Six

SVETAN *and* MENA.

*Pause; he refuses to meet her eyes, he's refusing to speak to
her.*

MENA. What's her name?

SVETAN. Lea.

MENA. Lea. Is that the wife or the child? Your wife or your
child?

SVETAN. Raina. My wife is called Raina.

MENA. Raina, Lea. Raina and Lea.

SVETAN. She was my wife. Not now.

MENA. You're divorced?

SVETAN. We live in different places.

MENA. But you're married? Still married. Do you love her?

He says nothing.

You would never say you loved me. I've waited all this time. I tried to trap you into saying it. I should have guessed the reason why –

SVETAN. That is not the reason.

MENA. I should have guessed, I should have –

SVETAN. That is not the reason.

MENA. Do you see her, the child?

SVETAN. She lives with cousins.

MENA. Yours or hers?

SVETAN. My life is not your book! My heart is not your book.

MENA. You don't love me. Do you love me?

SVETAN. It's just a word, Mena. It's – (*He means it's too big, complicated, a thing to express just like that.*)

MENA. A four letter word! That's what you mean – a four letter word!

SVETAN. No.

MENA. If you'd loved me at all you would have told me.

⎧ SVETAN. That I loved you?

⎩ MENA. That you're married.

⎧ SVETAN. You would say I had a girl in every port.

⎨ MENA (*in over this*). I bet you've one in every port . . .
⎩   I thought you loved me.

SVETAN. It's not simple like you want.

MENA. I thought you loved me.

SVETAN. One day I'll come home from sea and Lea will be all grown up, she won't know me.

MENA. I would love your daughter.

SVETAN. It's not simple like you want.

MENA. I hate your wife. But I couldn't hate your child. I love you, I can love Lea too. I won't let you go.

She moves away or he does.

(*Promising herself, not him.*) I'll marry you. See if I don't.

SVETAN (*to himself, not her; in Bulgarian*). I married Raina because the kid was mine. Now we're all paying the price. Nobody's fault. I went to sea; she went to other men. Whatever happened this time, I'd be 'The klondyker looking for a passport'. Suppose it was true? *Became* true? When would I know? When my daughter gets a visa, or doesn't get a visa? . . . When Mena's first baby's born? . . . Sure: I love her; I don't want to let her go. But love and marriage, they're not simple like you want.

Scene Seven

MENA, BRIT.

BRIT. Don't be such a sap! What did you expect? He's handsome, he's – what? Ten years older – what did you expect?

MENA. He isn't married! He isn't – not really!

BRIT. You never asked.

MENA. Why should I? He never talked about –

BRIT. In Bulgarian?

MENA. He speaks English now.

BRIT. You never asked *now* either. I could feel sorry for the guy!

MENA. Whose side are you on?

BRIT. Mine!

MENA (*thinking of* SVETAN, *has stopped listening to* BRIT).
If I had a child, I wouldn't leave her, either. I see why he
can't say yes – or no. All he has to say is: 'I have to bring
my daughter' . . . Maybe she won't like me –

BRIT. Oh, it's settled – you're an item?

MENA (*ignoring this*). – Maybe she looks like her mother. I
hate his wife. I don't hate his wife, I'm afraid of her, I'm
jealous; she must be good looking –

BRIT. Jesus, Mena, shut up! Colonel Bogey practically
threatened to do you in, and you're humming the wedding
march.

MENA. Look, if Svetan was married he'd –

BRIT. Svetan IS married.

MENA. – if he was married to me –

BRIT. That'd make him bullet proof?

MENA *has no answer to this.*

It takes a helluva lot to scare Natka.

MENA. Svetan's not scared.

BRIT. Svetan's bloody terrifed!

MENA. He's terrified of going back to Burgas.

BRIT. He's terrified. Full stop. All three of them are terrified.
They jump at shadows, they won't go out alone. They're
squeezed to death between a very nasty rock, and a very
hard place.

A silence. Now the fear's declared they can feel it strongly.

MENA. Has chef made Hoover's birthday cake?

BRIT. Yes.

MENA. I'll go and ice it then.

MENA *goes.*

BRIT (*calls after her*). No marzipan! . . . (*To herself.*) He's
always telling chef to cut out the marzipan.

Scene Eight

MENA, COLONEL, BRIT, NATKA.

*Dark rainy (February) night. Not all the quay lights are
working. Very, very faint background music heard (off) from on
board.*

MENA *crosses the quay from pub to ship, shielding birthday
cake and/or parcels with an open umbrella. She has a little
toy/party trumpet. At the gangway she stands (poses, really):
blows the trumpet, waiting for someone (preferably* SVETAN)
to come and lower the gangway for her.

MENA. Ludmilla, ahoy!

*She blows the trumpet again, she twirls around, cake,
umbrella, and all – and so catches sight of someone (the*
COLONEL) *in the shadows. He steps forward, she starts,
drops some of her stuff.*

COLONEL. Good evening.

*He picks one of the parcels up, hands it to her – or tries to
– but as she fumbles and drops it, she steps back, stumbles
very near the edge (between ship and quay). The*
COLONEL *pulls/catches her.*

COLONEL. Hey – I save your life!

She's frightened, unable to shout.

Easy to slip, um? – Don't call out! – So dark here tonight.
Strange how many lights are broken. Vandals! Even here!

She starts to call out.

Please: don't shout. Afraid of me? (*Tutting.*) No, no, no –
you have to get used to me, Mena.

In the pub, BRIT, *with stuff for the party also, looks out the
window across the quay. Barely sees, but tries to make out,
the figures in the rain.*

BRIT (*she's not calling out to* MENA, *she knows* MENA *can't
hear*). Mena? – What's going –

The COLONEL *picks up something of* MENA's: *parcel or cake.*

COLONEL. You and your special Kralev can go anywhere you want – anywhere in the wide, wide world – but some day, I'll be there. Back door, front door, car door, garage door –

Suddenly he thrusts the parcel/cake at her.

COLONEL. Here.

BRIT (*calling out, hopelessly*). Meeeena!

But MENA's *like a rabbit in headlights, can't move, not even her arms. Except, inadvertently, to step back a pace – again coming dangerously near the edge.*

BRIT (*calling – unheard – to* MENA). Mena, run! – Run!

During this NATKA *appears – the opposite end of the deck from* BRIT. *The others do not see her. She is stunningly dressed (for the party, for* HOOVER*). In the dim lights she appears like the ship's figurehead, extraordinary, strong. None of the others see her.*

COLONEL *takes* MENA's *arm 'protectively'.*

COLONEL. I save your life again! If you fall down there –

NATKA. He-e-e-ey!

The call is long-drawn out, almost a yodel or ululation (as in some Bulgarian folksongs). It's the quickest, most effective – the only – way NATKA *can make herself heard and cut into what's going on. She's not only warning* MENA *– but the* COLONEL *too, she knows what he's capable of.*

The COLONEL *turns, startled momentarily, to look up at* NATKA. *At that moment* MENA *shoves him with all her might – she hasn't enough strength to topple him on her own, but he stumbles over a rope-ring/capstan/birthday cake, and slips/falls over the edge of the quay, into the gap between ship and quay.*

Immediately, she's petrified. She bends over the gap, it almost looks as if she's intending to help him out.

NATKA (*another blood-curdling drawn out cry*). He-e-e-ey!

> MENA *steps back a few paces* (*which is what* NATKA *intended*). NATKA *moves forward to look over into the gap below.* (*She doesn't lean over the rail and peer – she stands up straight, looking down without emotion. She's checking for any sign of life, recovery.*)

> *Below deck there's a burst of music – Bulgarian music, some noise from the party. The girls don't move.* MENA *and* NATKA *continue to stare.* BRIT *walks slowly from the bar over to the quayside.*

> *The Bulgarian music – strange, eastern lament – either played on the fiddle, and/or sung by the men, soars louder and stranger as the lights go down.*

CODA

SVETAN *on the phone.*

SVETAN (*desperate and afraid, rather than angry*). Why are you doing this to me, why, what's the point? Don't you see – now I'm forced to prove breakdown and adultery . . . Of course I can prove it! . . . No, I don't want to prove anything, only I need a divorce, for God's sake, Raina, can't we just go our separate – scared? *You're* scared! What the hell have you got to be scared of, Raina, I'm trapped here between the devil and the deep – . . . Who told you they could do that? Who said – they wouldn't do –

She's hung up.

You're scared. We're all scared.

*

BRIT *and* MENA . . . NATKA

As (*and before*) *they come on, sounds of laughter and maybe their conversation* (*blah, blah, better if these first words are barely distinguishable*).

M. It's ridiculous –

B. – What? –

M. The colour!

B. Ten percent off!

M. There's hardly room for a passport, let alone –

B. Bikini? Smalls?

BRIT and MENA appear, BRIT brandishing a small, highly coloured, rucksack.

MENA. I know you're travelling light, but –

BRIT. Where I'm going it's hot. Hot! And if it isn't hot enough I'll move onwards till it's hotter.

A pause. MENA suddenly realises BRIT really is going. Doesn't want her to go.

BRIT. Why won't you come? (*It's not the first time BRIT's suggested this.*) Just for a week or so, till I start my job? You could do with a break, now the inquest's over.

MENA. Svetan hasn't got a passport.

BRIT. I wasn't thinking of playing gooseberry.

MENA. And we need what money we've got. It's going to take forever for the divorce to come through. Forever and ever.

BRIT. Just have to go on living in sin.

MENA. Suppose they send him back?

BRIT. They can't send him back.

But they both know this can happen anytime.

They have to consider his application – and Angel's. The Unions are making bloody sure they do – and the Church – not to mention almost the entire population of Shetland. People are already whispering about where to hide them.

MENA. They can't hide forever –

BRIT (*in over this*). Stop being so bloody miserable. It doesn't help him any –

MENA. – I'm afraid. I'm afraid.

BRIT. *You're* afraid! Christ! What about Svetan? What about Angel?

MENA (*in over this*). What if I call out in the night? In my sleep? I have nightmares all the time. If Svetan hears –

BRIT. Everyone talks rubbish in their sleep. Everyone has dreams, bad dreams.

MENA. But if he found out, if he knew what really happened?

BRIT (*coming in on this very sharply*). It was an accident. 'Death by misadventure'. It's official. We weren't there, we didn't see – *that's* official.

NATKA *has come in. They don't see her.*

MENA (*not talking loudly here but loud enough*). I killed a man. I killed him.

NATKA. You wish you hadn't killed him?

They are both startled, guilty – they should have been more careful where they had this conversation.

(*After a pause when* MENA *gives no reply.*) You wish someone else had killed him?

MENA. He was going to hurt Svetan – me – you – all of us, even Hoover.

NATKA. If he was out there now (*With a nod or gesture towards the pier.*) would you do it again?

MENA. Let him drown? Yes.

NATKA (*in over this*). Kill him?

MENA (*full admittance, responsibility*). Yes. YES.

NATKA *instantly gives a yell, or cries 'yes' also, coinciding with* MENA's *second cry. With a kind of triumph. But she's deadly serious.*

NATKA (*to both girls*). Now: forget about it. Except for a little bit here (*Gestures/touches her own head, or* MENA's, *or* BRIT's.) to always, always guard what you say. No more talk. Never.

MENA. He feels – trapped. Waiting, waiting. If he knew *I'd* trapped him here –

NATKA (*in over this*). Of course he feels trapped. Stuck on this rock. A little job he doesn't like, every morning, eight o'clock. He needs to go to sea!

BRIT (*softly*). Oh, shit!

MENA *gobsmacked.*

NATKA. When he has papers again – then he can go to sea. And everything will be all fine, okay.

MENA. But – we're going to be married.

NATKA. Sure. But if you want him to be happy, he has to go to sea.

BRIT. He'll come back again. Like the herring –

MENA (*in chorus with her*). – Herring! I know! (*To* BRIT.) Easy for you to say.

But she's absorbing the advice, paying heed.

(*To* NATKA.) Hoover's never gone that long.

NATKA. Ah, but we're going – one day soon. Soon as we've bought a little boat. Hoover's never been South. The most beautiful wind in the world is the South East Trade. Flying fish. Blazing stars . . . It was brave, what you did. For love. But you have to give him more.

MENA. The sea.

NATKA. The goddam beautiful sea.

*

ANGEL *on the phone.*

ANGEL. Hello? Hello? Aunt Geni? It's your little Angel here . . . Fit as a Shetland fiddle, Geni! And you? . . . Good. That's good. And Mama? . . . Like you say, Genie, as long as she's grumbling, she must be okay. Did you get the coats? . . . The COATS? . . . They're quite something, aren't they? . . . No, no – no, they didn't, not too much – anyway, we're allowed to get a job after the first six months, while we're waiting for asy – (*Stops himself.*) Anyway, I've got a job –

But GENIE *has something more important to talk about.*

From the courts? Again? . . . Don't worry. They aren't addressed to you, it's me they want in court not you. No – no, don't tear them up. For God's sake, don't do that. Just keep them in the cupboard. Keep them as if I – keep them for when I come home – I don't know when. How could I look after you both if I was in prison? Or sweeping the streets – like Minko? At least I've got a job here, I can send you money.

GENIE*'s questions are upsetting him.*

I don't know when. Not for a long time. Don't tell Mama . . . Genie? . . . Are you there? Did you get the shortbread – Don't cry . . . Don't tell Mama, not until you have to . . . Sure, I'm okay, I'm okay. I'll phone on Sunday. Same time, Sunday. Don't cry. Love to Mama. Love to you.

He pulls the phone card out from its slot, walks out towards the quay.

The End.